TRADITION WITNESSING THE MODERN AGE

An Analysis of the Gülen Movement

TRADITION WITNESSING THE MODERN AGE

An Analysis of the Gülen Movement

Mehmet Enes Ergene

New Jersey

Published by Tughra Books

26 Worlds Fair Dr. Unit C

Somerset, New Jersey, 08873, USA

www.tughrabooks.com

Library of Congress Cataloging-in-Publication Data

Ergene, M. Enes.
 Tradition witnessing the modern age : an analysis of the Gulen movement / M. Enes Ergene.
    p. cm.
 Includes bibliographical references and index.
 ISBN 978-1-59784-128-3 (hardcover : alk. paper)
  1. Gülen, Fethullah. 2. Islam and politics--Turkey. 3. Islam--Essence, genius, nature. 4. Islamic religious education. I. Title.
 BP80.G8E74 2008
 297.092--dc22

                                                                2008021229

Printed by
Çağlayan A.Ş., Izmir - Turkey

CONTENTS

INTRODUCTION

This study is an effort to understand how the Gülen movement, named after the prominent Turkish scholar Fethullah Gülen, has a sphere of influence on the global scale. Active in more than a hundred countries with schools and intercultural centers, the Gülen movement is considered to be one of the most significant social movements that arose from the Muslim world.

Following some very diverse waves of propaganda after September 11, there is a growing interest in Islam, as well as in Muslims and Muslim social movements. Islam's encounter with the West has once again been experienced in relation to violence and terror—that is, within a framework of crisis. The charismatic, eminent, and opinion-leading personalities—as well as their political, social, cultural, and religious activities—have become the subject of many analyses. The waves of unjust propaganda directed at Islam and at Muslims have been reflected in a negative manner in the political and cultural relations between Western countries and their Muslim counterparts. Some world media outlets present Islam as an aggressive worldview which is often depicted as being equivalent to violence and terror. There is a psychological campaign to paint a picture of Islam as monolithic, as being against democracy and pluralism.

"The New World Order" concept makes it possible to position this reality in a context. The perpetrators of contemporary events will never be known. The small amount of credible knowledge about such events makes the picture incoherent, and scenes of international conflict thus tend to paint a false picture. It is impossible for the masses to gather complete and correct information. When we observe the wave of systematic propaganda carried out against

Islam, we see that the Cold War did not end—it merely changed direction. While my intent is not to speculate on new international concepts, there are many who are trying to fabricate a new concept—"the clash of civilizations." The civilizations that are destined to clash, so the story goes, are Islam and the West. The majority of international commentators see these events within the New World Order concept of some in the USA. We shall all see whether or not this is so. The USA is clearly engaged in a refined project to play a major, if not primary, role in shaping world events. Suspicions, conspiracy theories, and political crisis analyses proliferate, and Islam resides in the middle of this new world agenda. It is in this context that the importance of studying Muslim social movements continues to grow. I treat the subject within the context of wider international relations and, thus, some of my expressions and comments have to be viewed on a global scale so as not to be perceived as conjectural, redundant, or incoherent remarks.

One of the difficulties in studying Islamic communities and movements is the failure to discern circumstantial rhetoric of a community from its theoretical traditions and internal dynamics. Because of this problem, Islamic communities and movements are often accused of having a hidden agenda. If we read such cases incorrectly—or worse, if we do not see the differences at all—analyses will become subject to manipulation on different fronts.

Turkey's relations with its different cultural, religious, and ethnic components have been problematic in many aspects. Turkey comes from a long and wide-reaching historical experience; nevertheless a social order that guarantees peaceful pluralism has not been possible in this country. In problematic and fragile democracies like Turkey, the arguments and beliefs of religious communities are formulated with a certain worry concerning legitimacy. In truth, all movements that start with a concern for legitimacy follow the same path. There's nothing remarkable about that. But the problem lies here: when official ideologies are represented as a sort of "political faith," and when people are required to express their affirmation openly, everyone is continually subject to scrutiny about their intentions. This means that when the system closes itself off to certain circles, certain beliefs, and/or certain schools of thought, whatever legitimate arguments arise outside "the official line of thought" will be considered detrimental.

This problem is not unique to Turkey. Throughout the Islamic world, the same problem emerges between the establishment and Islamic communities. Such an environment creates a paranoid understanding of democracy. Naturally, if there is a gap between the social arguments and the basic principles that emanate from a particular movement, this has to be closely investigated. A sociological analysis of a social movement has to look at its intellectual, faith-based, and cultural references as well as its traditions, its internal dynamics, and its discourses of legitimacy. First and foremost, analysts must account for the fact that the basic reference for the intellectual and activity sphere of Islamic communities is Islam. What is important is how these communities perceive, interpret, and apply these Islamic references. It is also important to observe and analyze how they relate these Islamic references to contemporary social values, modern civilization, international cultural processes, and different worldviews. This study focuses on the Gülen movement in just such a manner by offering a threefold categorization. Aiming to show that the Gülen movement is not merely a religious organization, I point to its sociological, cultural and religious aspects; thus, I try to bring to light the movement's socio-cultural identity alongside its religious one.

In the first chapter I cast a general look on Fethullah Gülen's personality and mission. This study is obviously not a biography of Gülen. While an all-encompassing biographical study of Gülen, a person with many aspects, would surely be a worthy endeavor, such a study is well beyond my intellectual aspirations at present. Biographical studies tend to be efforts that start with the principle of hoarding all the life material into one book, while taking care not to leave any information aside. Analyzing a personality such as

Gülen may be more difficult than analyzing a movement. Gülen is a representative of the *ulama* tradition—a body of scholars who have taken on the responsibility of transmitting the Islamic heritage to future generations; there is a discussion on this tradition under the "Political Islam or the Concept of Islamism" in the second chapter. Gülen is a person who has witnessed several fundamental transformations of the modern age and who has a deep spiritual and social identity. As I argue below, Gülen's life and work ought to be analyzed by scholars who concern themselves with international movements. In this regard, he is an ideal example to study, for he has inspired a global movement that stresses reconciliation, tolerance, and respecting everyone as they are at a time when the modern age is encountering Islam and Muslim culture around the world when the relations between civilizations are becoming strained. Fethullah Gülen and the movement he has inspired offer the world a new Islamic perspective for the West to ponder in a post-September 11 world.

Another dimension of the Gülen movement I would like to expound on in the first chapter is the oratory tradition. The transmission of knowledge through oratory tradition is among the most important socio-cultural manifestations of Islamic society. In Islam's history, sermon and address developed as a literary art form; it is one of the ways by which Islamic cultural heritage passed on to future generations. Gülen's early religious and social activity found expression in this oratory tradition. Gülen first attracted the attention of the public with his oratory power, which contributed greatly to shaping the movement. His speeches activated mechanisms of knowledge as much as they stimulated people's emotions. That is to say, he was an orator who spoke not just from the intellect, but also from the heart. For this reason, Gülen has to be considered within the legacy of oratory tradition, in addition to his writings and social activities. Accordingly, I analyze the role of this tradition in shaping Islamic communities under a separate heading. We can see the traces of this oratory tradition in the socio-cultural structures of Islamic communities in the modern period. When we grasp the social effects of this tradition, we are able to understand how the words and advice of an opinion leader like Gülen manages to generate such great influence on the masses. Gülen is not an active member of the hierarchical structure of any organization, and thus we have to seek the reasons for the wide-acceptance of his words, ideas, and advice in the traces of this long-lived oratory tradition. Since the significance of this tradition is not well-known, time and again, Gülen has to explain that he has no connections to the community or to its establishments in any organic sense.

In Islam, the sensibility of "benevolence" meets with other social ideals to produce a wide-reaching influence. This is the function of oratory tradition. For this reason, Islam is a religion that is open to countless diverse perceptions. That is precisely what makes Islam universal. Gülen calls upon and stimulates the feelings of benevolence and tolerance of the Turkish Muslims. The epic-like self-sacrifice that exemplifies the Turkish people in this movement provides a clear and endless program for grasping Islam. This is where Gülen's mission gains importance. Like a maturing child, sometimes a society looks to acquire everything it can, only to squander all that it earns. Turkish people are remarkably generous and benevolent. Gülen has gleaned this sense of benevolence, and has warned his followers not to squander it; instead they should direct it to high social ideals. He has thus produced a new model for human being and a new system of social self-sacrifice.

In the second chapter of my analysis, Sociological Perspective, I approached the concept of community with some focus on its manifestation in both Western and Islamic thought. Although I tried to carry out an analysis that takes into consideration the social circumstances that paved the way toward community formation and its consequences, my primary goal is to contribute to a discussion of this movement by focusing principally on its method of engagement. The chapters in this book are complex and multi-faceted; each could be the focus of separate studies.

I believe that neither religious argumentation alone nor specific discourses from social science have the necessary explanatory power to provide a satisfactory analysis of the phenomena of modern Muslim communities and movements and the way they come into being. One of the basic reasons for this incapacity is that discourses across the social sciences originate from Western material and social conditions. In fact, this also has to do with the more general problem of how Islam is perceived in the West as a religion, culture, and civilization. Thus, the problem moves beyond analysis and method. For this reason, my approach in this book draws on both religious argumentation and social science discourses. I have taken the liberty of not confining myself to any standard academic genre, thus the content does not follow a specific discipline, which may not be very appealing to academic circles. The content presented here is an outcome of not an academic goal that I pursue, but of many concerns that I feel with respect to recently bourgeoning studies analyzing the Gülen movement. The content therefore has been shaped to serve as a preemptive to encourage researchers to come to a realization of the inner dynamics of this movement and numerous multidimensional factors that converge in its formation before they operate social analytical paradigms. Otherwise, I have worries that this movement may face the same fate of misinterpretation many other Muslim-based movements and communities have suffered. Even though this may lend a discouraging aspect to my study, my aim is to leave everything that can be said about the points of discussion and the concept of community open-ended, to make space for further research. Apart from that, I want to stress that individual discourses are not able to present a sufficient analysis on their own. Should this study provide a basis for, or contribution to, a deeper study, it will have served its purpose. The point of this opening caveat is to suggest that because the concepts incorporated are largely untested, this study is open to criticism, as well as suggestions.

Principled studies on Muslim communities in Turkey and in the world do exist; however, books cannot say everything. It is also not right to clothe all these movements in the ideas one gleans from such publications. Books are no more than extended comments based on observations from particular viewpoints. No single study can explain the whole of a community or movement's social existence. To wholly understand a religious community or movement, a researcher must focus on its religious, social, and cultural *raison d'être*. This is precisely why I refer to this study as "an attempt to understand," rather than a definitive explanation.

The third chapter, Cultural Perspective, is devoted mainly to the educational and intercultural dialogue efforts of the Gülen movement. With an introduction discussing topics like rationalism, objectivity, positivism, progress, religion, and metaphysics in the Western thought, this chapter explores Gülen's emphasis on renewal in education with a transition from *madrasa* to college, the mission of the Journalists and Writers Foundation, and his overall philosophy on Islam's encounter with modernity.

Undoubtedly, this movement has a religious identity that is discussed in the fourth chapter. When we look at its structural characteristics and its global activities, however, we see that it also has a very wide vision and socio-cultural identity. The stress that we lay upon its religious identity centers on the Gülen movement's Sufi character although it is important to understand that it is not a Sufi "order." This soft and humane character flourished on Anatolian soil in a process that began when the Turks first encountered Islam. As it pays special attention to the early Anatolian Sufi movements, the Gülen movement focuses on the project of dialogue and tolerance based on an Islamic Sufi precept: respect for humankind and the created. The Sufi movement is a wide-reaching social phenomenon; it dates back to the first centuries of Islam and has produced various sorts of institutionalized brotherhoods that vary in regard to the political and social conditions. The Gülen movement does not have a particular context or organization a typical Sufi order would have; nevertheless, Gülen's approach gives a higher priority to, and is thus principally in tune with, the thousand-year-old social fabric of Anatolian society.

When analyzing the internal and spiritual dynamics of the Gülen movement, I argue that it exemplifies a reproduction of the historic Sufi tradition that is compatible with contemporary social conditions. When mentioning the spiritual life of Islam, I empha-size that the essence is the Sufi tradition that comprises the princi-ples of asceticism (*zuhd*), piety (*taqwa*), and excellence in virtue and beauty *(ihsan)*; and in this work, I aim to highlight the direct relevance of these Qur'an- and *Sunna*-based concepts to the Gülen movement. Even though these terms have experienced a semantic transformation in their course through history, I do not have space in the current study to offer such a semantic analysis. For the pur-poses of this study, therefore, I use the general meaning of these concepts as they are used in Islamic literature.

Gülen's message is nourished equally by both his reason and his heart. In this way, we discover two aspects of Gülen: he is both a scholar (*alim*) and an insightful man of wisdom (*arif*). He is well-versed in religious sciences, Western culture and philosophy, and the current social and cultural problems of the world. We observe him in his identity as a rational thinker in all these fields, and as a scholar. Gülen illustrates great depth of insight and vast knowledge of Sufism, metaphysics, and the cosmos. In order to grasp or define Gülen's spiritual accumulations, one has to exert serious effort to become familiar with the dynamics of spiritual life and the concepts that guide his behavior. The Islamic-Sufi experience requires a high-er and a different level of conscience and sensibility; even an effec-tive analysis of Sufi terminology cannot properly transform the "experience of mysticism" into expression or discourse. At times, it requires one's direct experience with Islamic spirituality.

As a theologian, my intention is to highlight his level of knowledge in Islamic sciences, his capacity to infer judgments and critical interpretations (*ijtihad*), and his command of multiple disciplines. While expressing opinions about such matters is possible within the confines of language and culture, I refrain from analyzing aspects of his spiritual life due to the overwhelming challenge of doing a satisfactory job on the subject. As an individual, Gülen appears to be nothing more than a plain Muslim. However true this may be, he also epitomizes a life of high spiritual and metaphysical tension. People around him feel strongly attached to his presence, his way of addressing and expressions. He goes to great pains and is tremendously careful about his relationship with the things and beings around him. Wherever he resides, he has a strong mystical bond with his location, which illustrates the sphere of influence he has over others through his wisdom and character.

This study does not attempt to cover all the viewpoints, or the range of potential political, social, and cultural repercussions these viewpoints might have in on the Gülen movement. It does not purport to be comprehensive. It is quite limited in regard to its scope and the information that is presented. The theses in this book do not go so far as to produce a broad theory. There is, no doubt, a need for a much wider study that focuses on the social roots of this movement and the implications of its concept of community. Such a study could explain the broader potential impacts of this movement.

ACKNOWLEDGMENTS

I am indebted to Ihsan Yilmaz, Ahmet Kuru, Joshua Hendrick, Bernadette Andrea, Mustafa Gürbüz, and Hüseyin Şentürk for reviewing the manuscript before publication. Their constructive critique and editorial input have extensively contributed to bringing the text into its final shape. I appreciate their cooperation and am very thankful for the amount of time—every moment of which is very precious—they had to spare out of their numerous academic and intellectual work for reviewing this project. I am also grateful to Ali Köse, Nagihan Haliloğlu, Süleyman Derin, and Mehmet Fatih Serenli for translating most of the texts which were originally written in Turkish.

CHAPTER ONE

M. Fethullah Gülen and His Mission

M. FETHULLAH GÜLEN
AND HIS MISSION

THE CULTURAL FOUNDATIONS OF TOLERANCE
AND DIALOGUE

Because modern states are built upon urbanized societies, problems pertaining to humanity, society, and democratic values are complex and differentiated. All of our acts—be they political, economic, social, or cultural—work toward getting our share of the cake. Our minds cannot fathom acting without expecting recompense, of giving without taking. We are at the threshold of an age where "service to humanity" is facing extinction. This is the advent of a totally mechanical, digital world where all human faculties are headed toward annihilation. It is a fall from grace for humankind. Human beings are becoming a commodity, or a means of commerce, whereas they were once considered the universe's founding principle. The problem with the modern world is this sort of human. To counter this tendency, everywhere people are directing themselves to spirituality, to the divine aim that will remind human beings of their true value.

Some political paradigms purport that the institution of a multicultural, participatory, pluralistic democracy will solve all social problems. According to such paradigms, all problems emerge from the lack of such a system, and from the inadequacies of democracies and legal systems that are deprived of participatory and pluralistic qualities. The argument is that such inadequacies yield conflicts that come in the form of ethnic, cultural, communal, political, or ideological demands. Should democratic rights and institutions be established, and should such institutions serve all citizens, people would no longer be moved by ethnic, communal, cultural, or other like social affiliations. On the other hand, some people consider such problems to be marginal phenomena—simply a price paid for economic modernization. According to this view, the real problem is that some people feel left behind in the process of modernization. When these people reach a particular level of economic development and wealth, the story goes, they will stop being problematic and will integrate accordingly. Once people internalize "tolerance and mutual respect," as embedded within the concept of democracy, and once they made these principles sovereign in their personal and public relations, then social problems would dissipate, or so it was hoped. Reality, however, proved that even after democracy has been established, religious, ethnic, and cultural differences continue to be a source of conflict.

Today, there are 192 United Nations member states, and perhaps twenty more outside the UN umbrella. There are more than six hundred language groups, and more than five thousand ethnicities. In only very few countries do all citizens speak the same language or belong to the same ethnic-national group. Such political, social, cultural, military, and religious multiplicity signifies potential dissension and conflict on an international scale. This potential often makes democratic assumptions uncertain and debatable. Since the end of the Cold War, ethnic and cultural conflicts have become central rallying points for political violence.

These issues threaten the future of all people in the world. Thus, it is necessary to re-institute the cultural foundations of tolerance, understanding, and dialogue in a wider and more encompassing system that rises above old democratic practices. Naturally, there is neither a simple solution, nor a single formula to cure global ills. We should not fool ourselves. Many suggestions may work in specific conditions, but they can hardly be consistently applicable on a universal scale. If we can get rid of our prejudices toward other people and take into consideration different experiences, we may find that local movements may contain possible solutions to certain universal problems.

The ideology of modernization offered a human model, which was related more to the "individual" than to humankind. The modern person lived in a corner, alone and self-interested. Ideology equaled progress—to earn, and to exhaust the limits of riches and welfare. In a limited portion of the world, this model took root. But people were quick to see that even when they reached the spatial limits of riches and welfare, their political, economic and socio-cultural problems continued. And as material riches increased, spiritual poverty increased accordingly. Humankind reached a state that bred only material and spiritual dissatisfaction. People, masses, and communities started to question the system under which they lived, forming pressure groups and large organizations.

In the historical moment of social, economic, and political transformation, we see the *element of humankind* in the foreground. Human existence on earth and our way of self-realization are once again in question. The same questions that occupied the minds of early naturalist philosophers occupy the minds of philosophers today. In this moment, we also observe that faithful life and religious practices are on the rise around the world. After humankind's adventure with modernization, and the subsequent prices paid in all sectors of human organization (cultural, social, economic, and political), humanity turns once more to the divine for answers. It seems as though the broadest and most satisfactory answers to existential questions might be inspired by the concept of the "virtuous person," which has been depicted in the heavenly religions in different forms. .

There is a need, therefore, for a sustained effort to revive the real value of the virtuous person. The goal of this effort should be nothing more than reproducing the person of the people (i.e., the "person of tradition," the self-sacrificing, and spiritually equipped person). This calls for a generation that devotes itself to service. As an old Turkish saying goes, *"Hak için halka hizmet"*—serve humanity for the pleasure of the All-Mighty. Having freed its mind and conscience from such a spirit of devotion, however, the contemporary mind cannot grasp this sort of lifestyle. Yet individuals who possess such a spirit have played key roles in the establishment of human civilization, past empires, and states. Today, there are many sociologists and social engineers who strive to bring about just such a person. Indeed, modern civilization is in dire need of self-sacrificing spirits who devote themselves to community, and of a genuine movement for dialogue and consensus.

The mission of the Gülen movement is of great importance at such a juncture. Alongside the historical and social projection discussed in this section, we should also include Gülen's charismatic personage as a key factor that draws attention to this movement. Therefore, even though I do not intend to make a character analysis in this study, I think it is essential to touch briefly upon Gülen's biography.

WHO IS M. FETHULLAH GÜLEN?

Gülen was born in 1941 into a traditional family of five boys and two girls in the Pasinler district of Erzurum. His father, Ramiz Efendi, was a government-employed imam who performed his duties in various regions.

Erzurum lies in the northeast of Turkey, and it is socio-culturally very conservative. It is a town that has, for long centuries, reflected the basic religious and national values in its social make-up.

Gülen spent his childhood in an atmosphere of traditional dervish orders and religious schools (*madrasa*) that defined and perpetuated conservative values. He had an insatiable curiosity and a love of knowledge. Thus, it was impossible for the limited surroundings of his town to satisfy his intellectual desires. At a young age, he directed his mind and attention to cultural, political, and social events in the outside world. Gülen remembers that during his first years in the *madrasa*, from time to time, he would focus on social problems. As he grew up, he came to discover the world of art and intellectual activities of his immediate social world. He completed his *madrasa* education within a short time, but he never had an opportunity to receive an official education.

Those years were the years when the Turkish Republic had just lost its founder and had yet to build its institutions and establishments. Since the Ottoman Reformation (Tanzimat) period, the country had been, and still was, witness to many political, economic, and socio-cultural problems. The country's intellectuals experienced a fall from grace; they felt they were part of a defeated and lagging Islamic civilization. There were dozens of intellectual problems that were discussed over and over again. These problems had no obvious resolution and were left to the state to solve. The country's intellectuals were too tired to speak of even the simplest of matters. Issues having to do with Islam and religious social life already seemed long buried. Turkish democracy was fragile, oscillating between a single-party and multi-party system. Political and sectarian fights, inner feuds, continuous economic crises, poverty, and numerous other problems caught hold of Gülen's young mind. He thought of the Muslim world's two-centuries-long decline and tried to find remedies that could reverse it. Gülen revisited these problems through the perspective of contemporary cultural values. He thought it was imperative to filter the most essential elements of issues that had been lost in complex detail, in order to organize them once again to form new areas of will and enthusiasm.

In the last two centuries, two lines of thought were influential in the philosophical and political viewpoints that were put forward to explain and bring solutions to the decline in the intellectual and religious circles of Turkish society, and thus to facilitate participation in the world of modern civilization. One of them was extreme conservatism, and the other was based on rejection of the historical legacy—of both traditions and social practices. The latter preferred to join the world of Western civilization without questioning the process and freed itself from its traditional social identity.

The former interpreted the dynamics of progress totally within the boundaries of the tradition with a conservative mindset; the latter defined progress through the material and cultural values of Western civilization and the way of life these values produced. Naturally, there were those who proposed a third or a fourth way, and there were some who advocated a synthesis of the first two.

Fethullah Gülen Hocaefendi emerged from a traditionalist community. Accordingly, he progressed on a path defined by ready-made models and traditional norms. His close vicinity was not very likely to welcome new interpretations which would be considered "out of order." This is why his first initiatives encountered a conservative reaction. Gülen is a man devoted to traditional values. Over the years, however, he has never shied away from bringing traditional cultural values face to face with contemporary Western civilization. In that respect, his enterprise contains elements that bring new openings for the contemporary and the traditional in both theoretical and practical terms. From the first period of his religious and social activities up to his later educational activities, his mission has been to illustrate that religion and traditional cultural values, on the one hand, and scientific facts, on the other, do not contradict one another. On the contrary, they support one another and they can be put to the service of humankind in genuine harmony. Gülen has never hidden his religious identity. He has always acknowledged with self-confidence that he perceives this world to be nothing more than what he learns from his deep religious experience. He believes that religious identity and practice are not separate from humanity's social presence. In that respect, he has a worldview consistent with his beliefs. He stresses the idea that a genuinely sincere and religious character would benefit the state and the society. Contemporary thinkers have generally concentrated on the state, city, and economy. Gülen, however, has directed his attention to the *human being* that lies at the heart of all this. According to him, the most important problem of contemporary civilization is education. If the individual is virtuous, he or she will be virtuous in all things: the state, the city, and the economy. Gülen, however, does not consider the issue of the *human being* to remain a purely intellectual topic. He has transformed his considerations into a serious project of social practice.

Conservative attitudes tend to hold that in the face of new issues, following traditional precepts gives one more confidence. New ways of looking at things can be noteworthy to the extent that they are in keeping with the accepted arguments that have been formed in the past—that is, in the light of traditional values and norms. Such a perspective abstains from adding new interpretations and experiences. Gülen tried to formulate a new way of proceeding, a new way that has a firm hold on both the confidence that tradition gives and on the new social values. This was a greatly incorporative attitude.

As a young man, Gülen found himself in a position to deal with two different cultures, Islam and the West. Beginning three generations before him, people had experienced an identity crisis between these two cultures and civilizations. Gülen had a good view of the transforming cultural view of his age. Rather than falling into emotional or ethical despair in the face of social and institutional transformations occurring in Turkey and the world in general, he did not shy away from drawing on both individual and traditional experience while actively engaging with current social transformations by way of conscious participation. He developed a perspective that fed his personal, ethical, and cultural ideals with new repertoires of knowledge.

As early as the age of fifteen, Gülen entered an atmosphere thick with such thoughts, and he was a young man who had already matured in thought. Both the environment of his family and the conservative *madrasa* circle in which he grew up had led to this early maturation. Inside himself, he already had spiritual experiences, and his mind was rich with great enthusiasm and activity.

THE ORATORY TRADITION

A better understanding of the Gülen movement and its mission is very much dependent on comprehending the oratory tradition (*sohba*) in the Muslim world. Since the advent of Islam, the oratory (*shifahi*) tradition has been one of the most significant means for cultural nourishment and communication of traditional values. While the *madrasa* has been the means for systematizing religious thought, public speaking and oratory have served as channels to convey it to the public. The pulpit in the mosque has been the natural channel for this; the pulpit was the center for the production of popular Islamic culture and the stage where the Islamic art of oratory came into being in its original form and style. The mosque has been the most pivotal element of Islamic civilization and urban culture. It was a center of interaction for the town dwellers and huge urban crowds who went out for business, shopping, or for other purposes. The mosque has taken a central place in the shaping and molding of Islamic culture. The cultural environment from which Gülen originated was situated at these traditional crossroads. He is primarily a member of the *madrasa*. He has pursued a life that is very much interconnected with the mosque and the masses. The social manifestation of experiencing religious thought and the form of belief orbited around this centre. The *madrasa* was very much related to the mosque and to the social life of the community. When he first climbed the stairs to the pulpit in his early *madrasa* years, he was "not tall enough to reach over the pulpit," in his own words. From his early childhood, Gülen was a very sensitive and enthusiastic person. This enthusiasm later helped him develop a special oratory style of his own. His initial experience in his first sermons led him to realize how effective the oratory tradition had been across centuries, as well as its positive and substantial influence upon the masses. This art of oratory would shape his entire commitment and lifestyle. He devoted himself to the use of this art as an instrument for communicating faith (*tabligh* and *irshad*) and encouraging charity (*himma*) as an endeavor toward mobilizing the full potential of the society, religion, state, and nation. He seems to have adopted the Qur'anic verse, "Urge on the believers (to take their responsibility)" (Nisa 4:84) as a mission and symbol. In the historical sense, the "power of the word" would manifest itself once again in his elevated and spiritually powerful oratory.

His public speaking is probably the most outstanding of his many aspects. In fact, many people have come to know him only through his fervent oratory. His knowledge and scholarly interests in Islamic studies and modern Western sciences have been overshadowed for years by his mastery of oratory although his articles and poetry were being published in various magazines. For long years, he studied not only religious fields but also history, philosophy, sociology, literature, and art. However, all aspects of this absorbed knowledge would come to the surface either in molding the masses and transforming them into "teachers" (*muballigh*), or in other instances when they could be put into practice.

His official post commenced in 1959 after he passed an examination by the Turkish Directorate of Religious Affairs, and it lasted for about thirty years during which he served as an imam, a preacher, a teacher at Qur'anic schools, and in various management positions. He preached in many cities, including Edirne, Kırklareli, Izmir, Edremit, Manisa, and Çanakkale. During his professional career as an official preacher, he had close contact with the masses. In the true sense of the word, the art of oratory, which had been dead and forgotten for almost two centuries, was granted a revival thanks to his high enthusiasm, profound soulful and spiritual experience, vast knowledge, and comprehensive cultural grounding. In a most sincere fashion, and by virtue of his willingness, he has activated the religious, patriotic, and benevolent emotions of the masses by making use of all the delicate aspects of this skill. Hopes and enthusiasms have found a safe ground upon which to be rejuvenated with his sermons. Thousands, even tens of thousands of people, have rediscovered themselves in his addresses, and they have developed a feeling of confidence in themselves as well as in their societal values.

Gülen's first activity was characterized by his services as a traveling preacher moving from one city to another. Therefore, his preaching and his engagement with crowds have always been most observable. His style was shaped in accordance with the socio-psychological demeanor of the society he was addressing. He would filter all his actions and words through the most sensitive screens before he revealed them. He observed a most careful life, as if he were always under scrutiny. This alertness was a consequence not only of a concern for deserving the goodwill of the faithful community, but more due to his firm commitment to the dervish tradition in which it is observed, with a strong conviction and utmost sensitivity, that every word and action is under divine supervision. He has been a real modern servant (*abid*), ascetic (*zahid*), and dervish, and this accounts for the major motivation behind the sensitivity in his words, conduct, and personality, and in his acute alertness. The prudence, insightful character, stillness, and calmness which suffuse even the most insignificant of his actions, and perhaps even his inner soulful experience, are based upon his profound and conscious understanding of servanthood. Through years-long observance of spiritual practices under strict discipline and training, he has been subdued, purified, and calmed of any possible inclinations toward the indulgences which are prevalent in human nature. All his emotions are revealed only after they have undergone this discipline. While delivering a sermon, even at a peak level of emotionalism, he seems to possess a prudent mechanism and a form of consciousness which controls his conduct and inner excitement.

He establishes such a level of consciousness with his speech that his life before and after the sermon takes form accordingly. Appearing before an audience is like a birth pang for him. He is very attentive to not exposing any statement, thought, or even a breath, if it is not the right time for its birth. It is necessary to digest his oratory power and the delicate life he has threaded around it in order to get a complete picture of the influence of oratory culture upon the essential dynamics of the Gülen community. This movement has produced and developed its own cultural traditions, in both religious and socio-cultural terms, while remaining very much tied with the traditional system of values.

As Gülen extended his social contacts with the masses, he became more familiar with their social and cultural problems. This close contact placed him in a position where he had to encounter these problems and seek solutions.

As a result of this intellectual journey, he reached the conclusion that the major problem for Turkey, or perhaps even for the whole of human civilization, is the education of humanity. Having reached this conclusion in the early 1970s, when he became a director of a Qur'anic school, he began to attempt to practice a different method of education.

He was officially a preacher, on the one hand, but on the other, he organized classes and summer camps for students. In his sermons, he taught that, in our time, it was more important to establish schools than mosques, and he channeled the spiritual enthusiasm of the public. However, this policy was soon to be opposed by some conservative elements in his environment who were unable to calculate the long-term social results of educational projects and opening schools. For many years, from the pulpits or by other means, Gülen strove to motivate the people around him for accomplishing educational projects, mostly in the form of opening private secondary schools. At the same time, he made sure that these were conceived as civil initiatives by the government officials as a product of the societal and national spirit, with no political or ideological objectives. The institutionalization process for these projects has been a totally civil activity, indeed. It has never taken the form of ideological or political opposition.

During the 1970s, the ideological fights that shook the whole world affected Turkey deeply as well. Turkey became a battlefield of intellectual, political, and ideological currents. In such conflicts, tens of thousands of young people had lost their lives. In those years, Gülen managed to keep many people around him and the great masses that he addressed away from all these fights with great care and patience. In the 1970s and 1980s, Gülen was probably one of the rare preachers whose sermons were attended by an educated audience in large numbers, and of a wide diversity. By the beginning of the 1990s, the first educational establishments (primary schools and high schools) started to show their capacities, accruing successes in science competition Olympiads in Turkey and throughout the world. This was proof that these establishments solidified their bases and that they had become institutions practicing scientific truths. In other words, they had become the manifestation of the necessity and consistency of Gülen's education mobilization. As a result, Gülen became the focus of attention for politicians who were free of state bureaucracy, of people involved in fields ranging from academia to the art world and from the media to intellectual circles. The 1990s were the years of opening up to the outside world, and years that triggered a wide process of dialogue with people who are in the limelight in various fields. This effort started a process of dialogue the like of which had not been seen in the recent history of Turkey.

FIRST STEPS TOWARD DIALOGUE AND RECONCILIATION

Gülen initiated his vast civilizational dialogue project by gathering people together who represented different intellectual and living styles in Turkey. Many of these people were associated with various intellectual and social groups who had fought each other physically, in the true sense of the word, throughout 1960s and 1970s, and who later clashed ideologically and socially in the 1980s. Gülen started to invite these people to various meetings in the 1990s, and provided them with an opportunity to come together. At these meetings, many of these people met each other for the first time. People who had once drawn guns on each other, and people who had directed their political youth groups toward the demise of the other, had an opportunity to come together, to eat at the same table, and to exchange pleasantries. The first of these gatherings were little more than polite meetings. Undoubtedly, however, all who were involved felt a sense of excitement as they laid the new intellectual, philosophical, and social foundations of togetherness. Soon, this wave of excitement resulted in the momentous "Abant Meetings" that first started in 1998.[1] A cadre of scientists from different fields of study came together to develop a new scientific and intellectual plan of action for the future. These people came from a variety of cultural, ideological, and political backgrounds, and they all came together in one great intellectual effort: to form a mutual living space in Turkey. The initiative that began with Gülen and his team developed into a platform that incorporated people of science, thought, law, and politics who since then are directing the policies of the platform. Gülen is not actively involved in these meetings, but remains the honorary president of the Journalists and Writers Foundation, which has organizes and finances this platform and its meetings. The search for dialogue and reconciliation was institutionalized on the initiative of these intellectuals and thus gained a significant character.

THE JOURNALISTS AND WRITERS FOUNDATION

The Journalists and Writers Foundation was established in 1994 accompanied by intensive coverage by the Turkish media. The first dinner gatherings, which illustrated expectations of goodwill and the spirit of reconciliation, later gave birth to the "Abant Platform," which was followed by publishing activities. Those who participated in these gatherings started new personal friendships, and formerly opposing sides quickly realized the richness of diversity. Especially, the spiritual leaders of different religions set a great example of togetherness in difference. All participants expressed their strong support for dialogue. Many probably had not expected such a warm welcome, and they similarly did not expect that these dinners would some day transform into an attempt to cultivate dialogue between religions and civilizations.

Undoubtedly, Gülen's broad sense of tolerance, his foresight, and his reconciliatory attitude created a wave of excitement and hope that could not have developed otherwise. Here we cannot disregard the powerful spiritual effect of his sincere piety and deep attachment to religious and cultural values of the society. In both the media and in political and intellectual circles, Gülen's religious identity became a subject for discussion. Apparently, how a religious figure like Gülen could catalyze such social activity they could not comprehend. Because these people had confined Gülen to the mold of a classical mosque imam, a religious identity that they never really embraced, they never realized the potential of his message. They did not know that Gülen was well-versed in Western philosophy and social science, in addition to the Islamic sciences. Such people were unable to account for Gülen's ability to bring together different cultures in an attempt to find solutions to contemporary social problems.

The Gülen movement and Islam

It is important for me to underline that the Gülen movement is not an ideologically driven organization. Gülen is against the use of religion as a political ideology. It would be wrong to perceive the Gülen movement as akin to political Islamism. The colonial period was the major factor that transformed Islamism into an international issue. "Orientalism" was a political and ideological product of colonialism, and it targeted not only the Muslim world, but the less developed countries in general. This movement defined all cultures and civilizations that were outside the geography of Western civilization as being backward, barbaric, and exotic—as "Third World." Orientalism was an ideology produced in an effort to facilitate a cultural transformation that would assist the political, military, and economic expansion of the West. Thus, at its core, Orientalism was both exploitative and colonial. Islamist ideology was born, therefore, as a political identity opposed to exploitation. The present circumstances of our day are certainly very different than when classical Orientalism and Islamism appeared.

The current international juncture and action have abandoned many of the classical Orientalist foundations, and have begun to direct themselves toward more human-based, ethical, and universal values. This development has transformed Islamic movements around the world. No doubt there are still marginal groups that act with political and ideological concerns; however, such groups have no vision and are often weak in regard to material power, general support, and ideological organization. Thus, it would be wrong to brand all formations in the Muslim world as movements that act with the political concerns and that present a direct threat to international relations. This is especially true of the Gülen movement. The most basic dynamic of this movement has a religious, social, and cultural identity which is totally independent of any political or ideological structure. Throughout his life, Gülen has stayed away from involving himself in politics and has never sought political ends. He has never subscribed to a presentation of Islam as political ideology. In fact, he has underlined that such an attitude poses a genuine threat for the communication of Islam. He has voiced this opinion in his public addresses and in his books.[2]

In contrast to the most common misperception, the Gülen movement is not a solely religious movement. In order to read the Gülen movement correctly, however, we need to incorporate more than just social movement analysis. First of all, the Gülen movement is not a reactionary movement, and it has no relation to the alienated reactionaryism. The individuals at the center of this movement come from select circles of Turkish society. These selflessly serving individuals come from urban areas, and have a high level of education, and have imbibed modern and contemporary values. Just as their goal is not driven by a political ideology, the individuals who comprise the Gülen movement are not reactionaries against official state ideologies. They do not act out of feelings of deprivation, as in radical or reactionary movements. On the contrary, their relationships are based on consensus, dialogue, and tolerance. Their personal and social relations are rooted in the principle of positive action, as they seek to transform social relations by producing alternatives without disturbing the order, destroying forcefully, or overthrowing the existing system. In their efforts to broaden the horizon of existing social relations, the general ideal of the Gülen movement is to serve the *individual, society, and humanity.*

IS THE GÜLEN MOVEMENT A RELIGIOUS ORDER?

Even though the essential dynamics of the Gülen movement look similar to those of the classical Islamic tradition of spiritual orders in certain aspects, its organization is different with regard to producing civil initiatives and its way of acculturation. Max Weber's concept of "worldly asceticism" can help analyze the Gülen movement only to a certain degree. Instead, it is a movement that has been organized by civil dynamics. The Gülen movement is defined by *modesty, self-sacrifice, altruism, devotion, togetherness, service without expectations,* and *by a depth of the spirit and heart with no anticipation for personal gain for any intention or deed.* These are all concepts of Sufi culture, and these are also among the intellectual and active dynamics of the movement. But these concepts do not only relate to a person's own inner world, as in some Sufi orders; they are also directed to the outside, to what is social, to the same degree. In that respect, the awareness of religious depth and servanthood to God has more all-encompassing and social aims. Weber views such action as a "rationalization of religious and social relations." But even such a notion does not fully encompass the rational and social dynamics of the Gülen movement.

Religious orders are directed toward both the personal and the private. They make the individual grow cool toward the world and direct him or her to experience spiritual challenges at a personal level. Even though he or she is not removed entirely from social life, a religious order instills a rigid sense of discipline so as to allow little space for new openings. The Gülen movement differed in that it is inspired by a philosophy that is akin to that of Rumi (d. 1273), Yunus (d. 1321), and Yesevi (d. 1165), which is embedded in a wider social context.[3] It is like a contemporary projection of the message of these historical Sufis. In this projection, "religious motive" and "social action" work in great harmony. Just as elements of self-discipline mature the person, they make him or her a participant in shared aims in the social sense. Gülen's understanding of service requires a genuine spirit of devotion. This fits in with the ascetic definition of Weber, and yet it is a dynamic that is broader and has greater continuity.

Gülen invites Muslims to fulfill the pillars of Islam (daily prayers, fasting, charity, pilgrimage) by taking modern conditions into consideration. He instills a broad understanding of charity to include the gifts of time and effort, not just money; he similarly conveys the idea that prayer is not just for us, but also for others. Thus, taking these as his starting point, Gülen's definition of "service" becomes both broad and continuous, extending to national, human, moral, and universal values. It adopts a rational attitude toward the basic values of state and nation. When one speaks of a "person of service," one refers to a person with a vast heart who can embrace a wide perspective, selfless service, and devotion. And this requires a transcending love for religion, for nation, and for humanity. That is why Gülen frequently refers to those who are filled with such a transcendent love, and ready to face any challenges on this path, as "*muhabbet fedaileri*" (guardians of love).[4]

THE GÜLEN MOVEMENT, DIALOGUE, AND TOLERANCE

Tolerance[5] and dialogue are among the most basic and broad dynamics of the Gülen movement. These two concepts, first devel-

oped on a small scale, have turned into a search for a culture of reconciliation on a world scale. Today, the idea of different groups
peacefully living together is a philosophical issue that modern states
are trying to formulate. The international relations of past empires
were founded on conflict and war. Different civilizations were separated by thick walls, which were supported by political, ideological,
and religious identities. Inevitably, this led to conflict. During the
long Middle Ages, international relations were governed by a "law
of engagement," which allowed for little space to express religious
or ethnic differentiation. The domestic laws of states and empires
were not exempt from this philosophy. Throughout the Middle Ages,
humankind's struggle for civilization found expression in aggressive
and passionate conflict. Today, with new concepts brought by globalization, the search for dialogue between civilizations and cultures
has entered a new phase.

The Gülen movement is a clear example of this search, a search
that has reached international proportions. Gülen strengthens this
search with religious, legal, and philosophical foundations. One of
the basic aims of the global education activities is to form bridges
that will lead to dialogue between religions and civilizations. The
long-lasting wars of the past had to do with the problem of power
balance that reigned in the international relations of the day. This was
probably the case for all political empires and religious formations of
the past. But today, humanity is not in a position to shoulder such a
conflict on the global scale. According to Gülen, Muslims today
should not shape their own cultural, social, and existential identities
according to destructive values which are rooted in conflict and fight;
these are not aligned with the universal value system of Islam, in
which peace, dialogue, and tolerance are the basic principles. Today,
humanity is not in a position to bear a conflict on the global scale.

This is the principle that the Prophet Muhammad, peace be
upon him, practiced in Medina. The people of Medina were composed of groups belonging to different religions and cultures. For
the first time in history, the Prophet enacted a system of values that

aimed to maintain a peaceful co-existence of these religious groups. What these historical documents show us is that the reciprocal rights and responsibilities of different religious and cultural identities were clearly defined and a consensus was reached. According to this, non-Muslims would be free to practice their religions, their way of life, and their way of worship. No one was to interfere with their partners in a pluralistic organization in which groups had religious, legal, and cultural autonomy. Ali, the fourth Caliph, would formulate this pluralistic freedom in a letter that he sent to the governor of Egypt, Malik b. Ashtar, as a systematic legal expression. According to Ali, people who lived in regions ruled by Muslims were divided into two main groups: one "our brothers in religion, the Muslims," and the other, "our equals in creation, the non-Muslims." They both have rights to protection. In history, there has never been a culture that has been able to place "the other" on such an ontologically humane basis and thus to exalt them. This definition of Ali's stressed the Prophet's saying: "All humans are the children of Adam, and Adam was of the earth."

The interaction of early Muslims with neighboring nations and cultures was rooted in human and moral principles. Six centuries later, a similar development occurred. The Mongols who reigned in the Damascus region in the thirteenth century had taken Muslims, Christians, and Jews who lived under their protection as slaves. A Muslim scholar, Ibn Taymiyya, went to negotiate with the Mongol commander, Kutlu Shah, for the release of the slaves. The Mongols refused to release the Christian and the Jewish slaves along with the Muslim ones. The scholar responded as follows: "The war does not reach an end until all the slaves are free. The Christians and the Jews are under our protection, we cannot accept that a single one of them should remain a slave." Kutlu Shah soon agreed to set free all the slaves.[6] During the periods when Muslims adhered to the principles of tolerance and dialogue, they thus developed a broad and accommodating perspective that guaranteed the lifestyles and freedoms of various religious and cultural communities. The Ottoman Empire was a typical manifestation of this phenomenon.

Today, the Gülen movement advocates social pluralism, based on the principle of tolerance, on a global scale. Unlike pluralism in the past, which was limited by religious principles, today we need broader cultural and political bases on which to build. In order to produce such a culture of reconciliation, members of different civilizations have to make a positive contribution to these efforts. There needs to be a revival of such values so that shared and livable pluralism can be established on the earth. Only then will the efforts of the Gülen movement meet with the expected response on a global scale.

CHAPTER TWO

Sociological Perspective

SOCIOLOGICAL PERSPECTIVE

THE CONCEPT OF COMMUNITY AND FORMATION OF COMMUNITIES

In the discipline of sociology, the concept of community (*Gemeinschaft*) derives its importance and complexity from the appearance of the "modern industrial society" which, in the West, has led to the dissolution of traditional identity structures and social organizational forms. In order to understand the concept of "community formation" in the Muslim world, it is well worth touching on the differences expressed in the way it is treated in both Western and Islamic imaginations.

Both in the cultural and epistemological sense, and also in the sense of historical, material and social circumstances, the existential foundation of community was formed differently in the West and in the Islamic world. The way the concept was treated in the West primarily followed a two part line. The first of these was the line of Karl Marx (d. 1883), Ferdinand Tönnies (d. 1936), and Max Weber (d. 1920). The aim of early theorists was to grasp the destructive and transformative power of modernity on human individuals and groups. Again, almost all of them—especially the earlier sociologists, like Marx, Weber, and Tönnies—observed the transformative effect of modernity first hand. Marx tried to define the economic dynamics of this transformation through labor, capital, government, and city. Partly influenced by Marx, Tönnies analyzed the shifts from traditional social life and hierarchy to modern social life and hierarchy. Weber analyzed the forms of social organization that emerged in modernity and the effects of the modern metropolis on different societies.

In his study on "community" and "society," Tönnies incorporated his concepts as "ideal types." He treated the togetherness of "community" as the most characteristic aspect of pre-modern, traditional society. According to him, community is made up of three basic motives and loyalties: blood, bond, and neighborhood. The basic forms of these elements are family, village, clan, provinces, guilds, and professional and religious unions, the family being the strongest. Social relations in pre-modern societies developed on the basis of solidarity, support, and sharing. Whether it be through bonds of blood, as in the family, or through rural territorial bonds, as in the village, town or clan, all "forms of community" produced traditional values that were shared by all. This is precisely the reason why these values were strong. With the emergence of industrial society, however, traditional and rural communities began to unravel. Gradually, rational relations replaced rural and traditional relations based on solidarity, sharing and support. At this juncture, the new social form that Tönnies calls "society" (*Gesellschaft*) emerged in opposition to "rural community" (*Gemeinschaft*). In traditional communities, shared feelings of loyalty and everyday necessities brought about shared habits, traditions, and rural values. In society, individuals are strangers to one another; they are disconnected and independent from one another. In community (*Gemeinschaft*), by contrast, people are connected to each other despite all sorts of differences.

Another sociologist who incorporated the concepts of "community" and "society" was Weber. Weber added a more dynamic view of community than that of Tönnies. He stressed the continuity of community, and claimed that human beings always develop the will and awareness to group around shared ideals and interests. This will and awareness is present in industrial societies, just as it was present in pre-modern societies. Still, Weber maintains that the group organized in the form of a community will, sooner or later, lose its social existence in modern society.

Tönnies and Weber have exerted great influence over community sociology and analyses in both methodological and conceptual terms, not to mention the manner in which these analyses are conducted. The concept of community that is appearing again at the heart of modern Western cities still represents provincial roots, and the culture of run-down immigrant and working-class neighborhoods that have failed to integrate to the modern city culture. The sense of loyalty found in the phenomenon of "community formation" is derived from pre-modern human relations. Yet, blood and territorial bonds have reproduced themselves in the city in more abstract terms. In countries like Turkey, working-class neighborhoods that have not been integrated to modern life have a communal affiliation of "fellow townsmen" (*hemsehri*), which reveals itself in a warm and welcoming context. But sooner or later they will integrated to modern life.

COMMUNITY FORMATION: IDENTITY CRISIS AND THREAT

The new methodology of social science has the tendency to read social and civil movements in democratic societies as part of the pluralist paradigm. But when the issue comes to the political, social, and civil formations in the Muslim world, there seems to be no place for such optimism; most social movements in the Muslim world are subject to theories of identity crisis stemming largely from the economic and social ruptures in the society. The understanding of "plurality" weakens the assessments of movements in the Muslim world, and comments clearly take their cues from modernization theories. Theories of identity crisis incorporate a method of reading into the ideology of modernity. They consider movements of this kind as movements that emerged in a void created by modernity. Industrialization, urbanization, and rationalization represent the melting pot of modernity. This pot consumes all sorts of traditional structures, identities, and forms of organization within its framework of modernity and rationality. This approach was the way forward to consolidate both the central national state and the contemporary secular civilization.

In parallel to the tendency of modernization, many scientists have, since the 1700s, believed that religiosity would decline. Sociology, too, at first believed that religion was at its last breath in the same line as the positivist thinking. The *idée fixe* of the ideology of secularism that religion would disappear was based on the presumption that, along with industrialization, urbanization, and rationalization, religiosity would automatically decline. This represents the essence of modernization theories, for the most basic principle in modernization is secularization. With modernization, there came a rapid decline in church attendance in many parts of Europe. The pioneering theorists must have witnessed this decline. Yet, in the sense of "individual religiosity," these theories had no real currency. Despite a decline in church participation, individual belief did not decline during the industrial period: rather, it rose.

David Martin, for instance, is a contemporary sociologist who opposes theories of secularization as they are represented in social theory. According to Martin, there is no definite or satisfactory evidence for the assumption that secularization will spread consistently, and he demonstrates how in the eighteenth, nineteenth, and twentieth centuries, secularization theory served ideological and polemical, rather than conceptual, purposes.[1] In the year 2000, the ideology of secularism started to show signs of decline. Social scientists referred to this phenomenon as "the return of the sacred." These social scientists claimed that secularization had been a false prediction and that religiosity was becoming more apparent in new and fresh ways. Modernity and religion appeared to be compatible after all.

Regardless of the anti-secularization currents typical of the modern era, religion today does not appear as a mere vestige among rural and uneducated villagers. On the contrary, religion is on the rise among educated and successful urban people, the very people who emerged bearing the fruits of modernism and rationality. Today, in Japan, new automobiles are blessed in Shinto temples; in

Russia (the land of Marxism), masses of people flocked to the Orthodox Church after the easing of the regime.

In the 1960s, one of the most fervent defenders of secularist ideology was Peter Berger. Today, even he accepts that this ideology has collapsed. He argues modern secularism has not proven effective in improving the individual acts of people and ameliorating the general injustice in the world. Neither the great "the myth of progress," the incredible victories of natural sciences, nor the relative successes of revolutionary movements have been able to offer sustained solutions to those who suffer from material or spiritual deprivation. As a result of secularism's failure, religion's capacity for consolation has gained a new credibility in people's eyes.[2] In fact, both in the Third World, as well as in the European and Western worlds, religious movements have always existed. They are either stationary or on the rise; they are new or old, antique or modern. Many practicing believers were frightened by the all-encompassing nature of secularist ideology. Consequently, while some religious movements developed an attitude against modernization, most religious movements suggested that these processes of modernization and secularization encourage religious feelings rather than facilitate their destruction.

My purpose here is to draw attention to the fact that the rise in religious leaning does not necessarily involve a rejection of modernism. Moreover, in analyzing this rising awareness in the context of community formation, we cannot treat religion as an entity that threatens the modern way of life. Rather, we must assume that religion is an undeniable and indispensable part of our individual and social lives. If there appears to be a "religious problem"—and many claim that "religious violence and terror" point to such a problem—it can only be said that this arises from political, ideological, and radical ideals.

THE CONCEPT OF IDENTITY CRISIS

It is clear that modernization has created fields of threat concerning our personal, social, and political identity of selfhood. The rapidly globalizing world continues to disrupt settled local identities and cultures. It subjects local and national values to interrogation using global criteria.

New social paradigms treat the concept of identity within the framework of conflict and political-social crisis. They suggest that there is a causal connection between all sorts of crises and social identities, and they search for new routes. It can be verified sociologically that, to a certain extent, an atmosphere of social crisis has a relative effect on the construction of identity. The prolongation of political, social and economic crises weakens social unity and awareness. The feelings of trust and loyalty the individual has to the "whole" may also thus be weakened. The lack of norms, power and trust in which society wallows during atmospheres of crisis alienates society from its own values. Then, a social structure that Durkheim calls "unruliness" appears. This unruliness may bring about all sorts of value erosions. If this atmosphere widens enough to span all social and cultural areas, then we may observe a crisis of identity or self. Indeed, an identity crisis is a crisis of spirit and self. It is a process of alienation from the society and from one's self. The most immediate consequence of an identity crisis is the radical fall in legitimacy on the part of the governing elites and their institutions. This crisis of legitimacy grows with the current leaders' failures in political, economic and social fields.

When we apply this basis to the formation communities and social movements, we can follow a straight line of logic: such communities emerge during periods of economic, political, and socio-cultural crisis, and they formulate an identity alternative to the existing social and political identity. They tend to isolate their members and associates from the unity of the society and load them with an ideology of opposition. This ideology may spread at the grassroots level and transform into a political opposition, or isolated members might be manipulated by existing marginal political organizations. That is why oppressive and antidemocratic political systems and states perceive formation of new communities and socio-civil movements, as threats directed against the state.

It is true that most radical, marginal, and/or fundamentalist movements do aim to formulate such an alternative identity and ideology. These movements exhibit feelings of deep psychological pain, high expectations, and an attraction for the masses. These movements could well prepare the requisites of all sorts of terror and violence under leadership that sees these methods legitimate. That is why we have to be prepared and equipped at all times to take measures to counteract the widening of the political and social bases of violence. But these measures and fears of violence should never turn into a political paranoia.

The sociological basis upon which community-formation and the new civil-social mobility occurs is different that the conditions that produce radical and/or marginal movements. First, the identity formulated by these phenomena does not necessarily challenge to societal unity. On the contrary, expansion of mobility may add onto the society values that lead to a further widening and opening up of the society.

Here, let us have a look at the basic motives that lead to marginal movement mobility in the Islamic Middle East, including Turkey, and the countries of the Third World. In general, the political systems in these countries have been established and dominated by a group of elites leaving the masses outside the scope of political decision-making process. The legitimacy of the political systems and elite classes have always weakened or gained strength according to the performance of their leaders. Muslim countries forged their political existence on poor bases of legitimacy, and thus have always lacked the basic political and democratic capital that is needed to make up the foundation stones of a sound public system. It has led further into the use of force in order to continue to hold power and to perpetuate the political mechanism. Oppression in Muslim countries has profoundly affected the socio-psychological consciousness of the masses, which has led to the questioning of the political legitimacy of the ruling elite.

When looked at from the political angle, the gradual collapse of the Ottomans (and the Persian Islamic empire) gave rise in the Islamic Middle East to competing ideologies of nationalism based on ethnic and linguistic identities. These included three major forms of nationalisms: Turkish, Iranian, and Arabic. The formation of these new identities took their cues not from Islamic values but from pre-Islamic roots. Turkish nationalism, inspired by Ziya Gökalp (d. 1924), attained a form of pan-Turkism, which took on a persona that traced "Turkish-ness" back to the ancient Anatolian cultures of the Sumerians and the Hittites. In Iran, Shah Riza (d. 1980) revealed a pan-Iranism that emphasized the pre-Islamic Aryan-Persian elements of Iranian society. The Arabian experience incorporated the nationalism of the ancient Egyptians. Up till the 1980s, the nationalist project in each of these regions turned into a search for synthesis between these ancient roots and Islamic values.

In addition, the Islamic identity was shaped by other experiences in the Arab world. Arab nationalism before and after the First World War demonstrated Islamic, socialist, monarchical, and Western influences. In Syria, Iraq, and Jordan, secular and social Arab nationalism took on a monarchic aspect. In Saudi Arabia, on the other hand, the Wahhabi and Salafi identities came to the forefront. The fact that individual and social Islamic identity met such an impasse led to a reaction that stresses the Islamic global identity, an identity that is at times named political Islam or Islamism.

POLITICAL ISLAM OR THE CONCEPT OF ISLAMISM

Since the Middle Ages, there existed polemical views of Islam in Western societies, defining it as a terrorizing and deviating belief system. Until quite recent times, Islam was considered to be a heathen and idolatrous religion. The writings of European travelers who visited various countries of the Muslim world during the

Middle Ages resemble the figments of a wild imagination. In these texts, Muslims appear as lustful, heathen, barbarian, and deceptive. Even the powerful political sovereignty of Muslims was viewed as connected to their sexual powers and barbarianism. Lust, oppression, and barbarianism—these seemingly were the sole elements that made up the Islamic East.

In *The Divine Comedy*, Dante (d. 1321) sentenced the Prophet, peace be upon him, to the eighth level of hell. Many European writers and thinkers, including Machiavelli (d. 1527), Simon Ockley (d. 1720), Boulainvilliers (d. 1722), Diderot (d. 1784), Molière (d. 1673) and Voltaire (d. 1778) have also described Muslims, Islam, and the Prophet as lustful, inductive to oppression, and vulgar.[3] Even Pierre Loti (d. 1923), who was known to be a friend of the Ottomans, considered local women in the Muslim world as lustful, corrupting, and alluring. When describing Egypt under Napoleonic rule, Flaubert speaks of libidinous men who commit adultery with their concubines in the great squares of Cairo within view of the public. This is all strange when one considers the fact that Islam has been viewed as a religion that brings strict rules to male-female relationships. The obvious discrepancy between the image of Islam as a faith that brings strict limits to the libido, and the openly libidinous picture of Islam that the European travelers painted, seemed to raise no questions in the European mind. This is a profound symbolic indication of the lack of commonsense in non-Muslim interpretations of Islam and Muslims.

For Jocelyne Cesari, the reasons for this discrepancy should be looked for in the history that came about as a result of the conflicts between Islam and Europe in the Mediterranean after the Middle Ages. She argues that all the information about Islam is a product of a Eurocentric viewpoint which has been built on both political and religious contradictions that have existed for centuries. From the most personal mode of behavior to the collective, the reality of Muslims has been buried under stale descriptions that have been heaped upon it.[4] There is no need to heap information in order to fill up this section. Even these few paragraphs are enough to express that when it comes to discussing something concerning Islam, there is a great difference between the intellectual viewpoints of the West and the cultural foundations of Muslims.

The literature concerning Islam in Europe is, of course, not limited to travelogues. When we come to the 1800s, we see that scientific research into Islam began rather early. These studies eventually emerged into an organized system of thought: Orientalism. However, behind these intense studies, there was the constant awareness of the "other." This anthropological approach to Islam was not successful in relieving European conceptions of prejudices; on the contrary, it enhanced these prejudices and, in the end, it declared Islam to be the enemy to Western values and to scientific progress in general. Orientalism built a tradition of science and thought that was based on an ontological differentiation between the West and the East. It thus prepared a legitimatizing ideology for international colonialism during the eighteenth and nineteenth centuries.

One of the main arguments laid out by the Orientalist thinkers was that Islam considered all scientific research a sin, which categorized Muslims close to barbarian groups. While Ernest Renan's (d. 1892) account of Islam and Muslims might not appear a direct attack, it revealed Orientalist conceptions nonetheless. For Renan, Muslims are different in the sense that they hate science; they consider research to be unnecessary, futile, almost heresy; and they hate natural sciences, believing they play rival to God. Renan did not feel the need to prove what he wrote, and he was clearly no specialist in Islam. He was known for his work on Judaism, and he was first and foremost a researcher in Semitic traditions. However, his research also had strongly anti-Semitic aspects, and perhaps his none-too-neutral attitude toward Islam was informed by his anti-Semitic attitudes. In his well-known conference on "Islam and Science," he attributed the lack of scientific progress in the Middle East to Islam. According to him, of all the Semitic religions and cultures, Islam has concerned itself more with revelations and poetic enthusiasm than with science and scientific thought.

What Renan says, in fact, is more of a description of the Western Christian church's attitude toward the sciences in the Middle Ages. The rationalist attitude taken toward the church after the Renaissance and the Enlightenment has been deflected toward Islam through the writing of European travelers in Islamic lands, thereby producing a corresponding image of Islam.

Today, it is possible to see the deep traces of the Orientalist tendency in several Western analyses of the Muslim world. Western media is dominated by the presentations that propagate a chaotic picture of symbols and Islamic cultural concepts. Descriptions of violence and fanaticism are updated, and thus the Western imagination is provoked against Islam. Moreover, the media focus only on the symbolic dimension of Islam and the Muslim world, and on the political and ideologically fundamentalist dimensions. They never make reference to other components of Islam. Betrayed by various media, it is impossible for the public to understand the political games that are being played in Algeria, Iran, Egypt, Afghanistan, Turkey, and Iraq. As long as they do not have access to sound knowledge and information about Islam they will only be plunged into terror when faced with such images. The phenomenon of the rising Islamic awareness in the Muslim world today will be, for them, synonymous with international terrorism.

This viewpoint has been enhanced by some of the movements that have come from within the Islamic world: the Iranian Revolution, the crisis of the American embassy hostages, the assassination of Anwar Al Sadat (d. 1981), the fatwa against Salman Rushdie, the Arab-Israeli conflict, the Algerian and Afghani crises, and the recent situations in the Gulf and in Iraq, in particular. The Western media's handling of these issues pointed to new hostilities after the collapse of the communist bloc. With every international act of terrorism that has been associated with Islam, the so-called "clash of civilizations" thesis has gained strength. In contrast to

the heavy emphasis on Islam as a political actor, there is still little
scholarly interest in the theological aspects of Islam. This lays bare
the intellectual and ideological roots of the tendency in the
Western imagination that insisted, and continues to insist, on reading Islam at a political level.

Two aspects of the political Islam claim attention here. First,
under the influence of the great ideologies of the twentieth century, the movements of political Islam have tried to define Islam,
first and foremost, as a political system. Second, they consistently
employed a discourse related to, "getting back to the origins." This
was undoubtedly a new movement of thought. It favored not the
fourteen centuries of tradition, but the Islamic sources directly (the
Qur'an and the *Sunna*) and the way of life of the first group of
believers. Political Islam in this regard is defined as "Islamism";
the terms are treated as synonymous.

Both sociologically and cognitively, Islamism is a modern movement. Although its social base is composed of rural and middle-class
sections of society, actors generally emerge from urbanized popula-
tions. Receiving their education in modern schools, Islamists have
lived in close quarters with revolutionist, Marxist, and militantly ideological groups. They adopted political and ideological attitudes,
organizational practices, and modes of social opposition in the non-
Islamic countries, and they applied these forms to Islam so as to
develop a new ideological movement that we call Islamism. They
saw no problem in making use of Marxist, militant, or liberationist
discourses in their political programs. Sometimes the discourses and
the ideological polemics they produced veered off to a point where
they could not even be explained through Islamic principles.

The political Islam views Islam from the framework of the city
and contemporary politics. Islam was now more a political and ideological system rather than a system of heart-felt, spiritual, and
divinely transcending values. It had to say something concerning the
new values of consumption being propagated by the big metropolis—the world of the cafés, theatres, music. In short, it had to say

something about the set of values of the modern society and the city. Such an Islam was undoubtedly an Islam that the classical *ulama* and traditional Muslim society were not used to. The Islamists wanted their conception of political Islam to penetrate all fields, from the individual, to the social, to the scientific. It wanted Islam to resist colonialism in Palestine, Lebanon, Algeria, and Tunisia. In Egypt and India, Islamists sought to fight poverty and economic crises apart from colonialism; in Turkey and Iran, it was expected to tackle the problems of modernization. It had to address all political and social discourses developed by all factions, from the pretentious intelligentsia of the Middle East; to the tribal rural and local cultures in the Far East; to the Marxist, liberal, nationalist, and universalist ideologies of the West. Motivation through a belief in the afterlife, as can be seen in traditional Islam, became almost irrelevant. The result of this situation is that the belief in the afterlife lost its importance in ideological Islam; this made Islam more inclined to worldly pursuits.

Islamists tried to turn Islam into the manifesto of a reactionary ideology. While doing that, they did not want to base their ideas on the tradition of 1400 years. According to this Salafi attitude, classical, traditional Islam was no different than the static social structures of the Middle Ages. From traditional Islam, they thought, it was difficult to pro-duce systematic solutions to the problems pertaining to the nineteenth century. Consequently, Islamism stressed the first period of Islam and its original sources (the Qur'an and the *Sunna*). A group of these Islamists claimed that Islam was a system that preached essential principles only. This claim was proposed for the first time in the history of Islamic thought. Traditionally, Islam then brought detailed decrees to many specific issues. However, the Islamists oriented themselves not toward the entirety of traditional legal values that have stood the test of time, but to the original sources which they perceived as preaching only basic principles. Basic sources were reinterpreted in a way so as to stress human reason and entrepreneurship. In order to prove that Islam could develop modern concepts in the face of Western values, this was an attempt to read the Qur'an in a new, social, and political manner; for the traditional manner of reading did not give them the opportunity to deduce what they wanted from the sources. They reformulated many legal and political principles according to Western forms. It can further be said that what pertains to Islamists is their will to pre-sent Islam more as an ideology than a religion. This is what accounts for Islamism's emergence as a contemporary ideology within the context of urbanization, Westernization, and modernization and for the fact that it shares the socio-logical fate and foundations of other contemporary ideologies.

The rise of Islamic awareness should not be confused with radical political movements, however. It is a striking fact that the radical versions of political Islam have yet to build a social ground upon which their political ideals are built. The sociological foundations of these movements, rather than being religious and Islamic, are ideological, and they manifest themselves as a challenge to international imperial powers. Here, I assume that the insistency of seeking Islamic grounds for such movements is due to the rigid forms of Islamic attitudes which some Salafi movements in the Arab world adopt. These movements usually take Ibn Hanbal (d. 855) and Ibn Taymiyya (d. 1328) as their predecessors. The practical basis of Imam Ibn Hanbal's call for Islamic roots was the collapse of political and social morals in Abbasid society. Some who had to confront the threats that came from without effectively transformed this modest call by Ibn Hanbal into stricter attitudes. The demise of the Abbasid dynasty perpetrated by the Mongols, the wide destruction by Hulagu (d. 1265), and the conflicts that followed also resulted in a deep political and spiritual crisis. This multi-faceted crisis brought about a more obvious reaction which grouped itself into a particular school of understanding and interpretation around Ibn Taymiyya. This political and cultural environment was likened to the political and socio-cultural crisis that the Islamic world experienced before and after the First World War. The emphasis of all the

Salafis who favor violence is the same: that current ways of life lead to a sinful society and that political regimes have diverted away from Islamic essentials altogether. But Salafism that favors violence has remained quite weak and marginal in the overall picture of the Islamic movements. not been able to build a social ground upon which to stand. Hence, the rise or fall in Islamic awareness cannot be equated with the political aims of a group that is engaged in a political struggle.

A consciousness that goes beyond simple religiosity and worship would be more accurate when one speaks of the rise of Islamic awareness; and this is in keeping with the Islamic essence. This awareness is not necessarily a constituting of an alternative identity in the face of a social and cultural crisis. It is an attempt to transfer awareness and meaning to the identity that existed before and after the crisis.

The Gülen movement has, in that sense, been a blow to this relationship between the rising Islamic awareness and radicalism. The dynamics of the movement, now and in the past, have never been based on a purely political or worldly aim. Its foundational power brings about a high Islamic awareness and yet it never encourages the formation of a political party. That is why it is an exemplary movement where humane social values and ideals meet together to form a meaningful whole. I believe the success it has enjoyed in the field of education, in particular, is due to the solution it has presented to social problems that have been produced by years of deep cultural crises.

The Gülen movement offers a kind of "spirit of mobility" within which people from all sections of society can find something for themselves. That is what electrifies different groups of people. It is not like ideological movements that cry slogans and hold sway on the streets. Its social influence comes not from the streets, but from the fact that sincere individuals within it serve with a spirit of devotedness. One of the significant elements of the Gülen movement is that it bases itself on a model of a balanced human being. The institutions that it sets up are the results of an earnest "spirit of mobili-ty" that is exhibited in the name of humanity. This spirit of mobility renders the movement active and dynamic, and saves its participants from turning into a passive and powerless mass that has no say in its own future.

A MOVEMENT THAT PRODUCES ITS OWN VALUES

The Gülen movement did not rise upon the values of a past move-ment or period of crisis. The movement has produced its own appearance, structure, social and moral values, and institutions. No school of thought has had a dominant influence on the structural and religious-spiritual dynamics of this movement.

One cannot deny the way that the *Risale-i Nur* (Epistles of Light) has fed the inner dynamics of the movement both in spiri-tual and intellectual terms. The *Risale-i Nur* is one of the set of books written on Islamic belief and faith in recent centuries which has had a great spiritual-social influence over the masses in Turkey. In that respect, its influence over the larger community of Turkish Muslims is clear and evident. This set of books might not have the organizational framework that one can find in contemporary sci-entific works, but in the manner in which it treats the issues, and in the way that it offers fundamental solutions to human and social life, it affects the masses more quickly and deeply than other works. It not only stimulates belief and religious commitment, but it also inspires feelings of solidarity and cooperation. This is the contribution of the *Risale-i Nur* to the Gülen movement.

The social and action-related dynamics of the Gülen movement have been shaped around Gülen's strong spiritual character, his articulate teachings, and his broad sphere of social influence. That is what we mean when we say that "the movement originates from itself." It is true that the religious activity and mission of the move-ment is fed by Islamic awareness, historical traditions, and the past experience of Muslims. But, in order to present these different historical experiences and the values decreed by the essentials of the faith with a new face, interpretation, and action—and thus confront contemporary gains and experiences—one must incorporate wide scientific knowledge and have the ability to interpret and provide insight into contemporary practices. This is where Gülen's personal store of knowledge, experience, and intellect come into play. His teachings marry the past with the future—religion with social practices. He has never looked at the current situation or the indeterminate future without taking into account the heritage of the past. Below, we will try to interpret his idealizing of the Age of Happiness (*Asr-ı Saadet*).[5] This idealization, in truth, manifests his loyalty to Islam and the depth of his religious activity. On his part, the issue is not a mere interpretation of tradition, which would have amounted to narrow intellectual striving. Rather, his life completely represents the values he articulates. That is, he practices what he preaches.

As is with other movements, there is a tendency to compare the Gülen movement with other Islamic movements and to categorize it in the same group of Islamic groups. According to some Western analysts, the foundations of all religious radicalism are the Muslim Brotherhood in Egypt and the *Jamaah Islamiya* (the Islamic group or fellowship) in Pakistan. Even the revolution in Iran is considered to be a radical branching out of these movements. Most religious movements in the Islamic world are analyzed as if they share similarities with either the Muslim Brotherhood or the Pakistani *Jamaah Islamiya*. It is true that these two movements, the Muslim Brotherhood and *Jamaah Islamiya*, have been an indirect source of inspiration for the recent religious/political revival movements in the Islamic world; however, one cannot speak of a significant level of influence by these movements on Islamic communities in Turkey. The basis of the Gülen movement does not represent any economic class or ethnic group as opposed to some Islamist movements in other countries. The masses that it is based upon, vis-à-vis religious and social determinants, are neither oppressed nor excluded sections of society. It enjoys support both from the rural and urban sections of society, and its grassroots level is made up of individuals from the lower-middle, middle, and upper classes. The main actors of the movement are from the educated classes, individuals educated in big cities and first-class universities. They do not carry any feelings of vengeance against the governing elite, or against the socio-economic circles that are considered to be the carriers of Western values. That is why they do not display a radical severing, like "formulation of an oppositional ideology," as is observed in classical movements. In all fields, rather than formulating an alternative, it adopts the formulation of solutions, a formulation that is reconciliatory and open to negotiation. From the start, the Gülen movement has neither sought nor obtained a political identity. On the contrary, the movement has been criticized by some religious circles for staying outside of politics more than necessary.

THE EMPHASIS ON THE AGE OF HAPPINESS

Undoubtedly, one of the important ideals that form the Islamic social and historical consciousness of the Gülen movement is the notion of the "Age of Happiness." This ideal derives from the first period in Islamic history. This system of values is based upon the lives and practices of the friends of the Prophet. This short historical period is when the Sunni line of thought came into being; its consolidation was made possible by the ideal practice during that period.

The Age of Happiness was the period when the prototype predecessors of the Gülen movement (and the predecessors of similar movements) lived. This period was characterized by pure Islamic belief. In that generation, there was no means by which to consider a Muslim organization as political, ideological, or radical. Believers lived a moderate social life; it was a generation of pious and sincere people living in harmony despite a high level of poverty. The individuals who lived during this period were artless, simple, and selfless to the point of asceticism; they had strong attachment to their religious ideals.

In the Gülen movement, the ideal presented through the concept of the Age of Happiness does not correspond to a "going back," or to deferred feelings; it refers to a practice of Islam that is based on the fundamental principles of action and maintaining strong attachment to the spirit of Islamic conscious. In this context, the way the Prophet and his companions exemplified the Islamic spirit is regarded as the main source of inspiration.

INNER DYNAMICS

From the very beginning of this study, we have tried to express how some Western sociological perspectives are insufficient for studying an Islamic community or movement, for these approaches base themselves on theories of economic, political, and social crises that occur in the context of the modernization. Such theories may disregard the inner dynamics of a particular movement and apply the same analysis used for other movements. Most theories of social movements, be they religious, political, ideological, or civil, can be categorized as one or more of the following:

1. Reactionary
2. Traditional-conservative
3. Reformist
4. Revolutionary and separatist
5. Expressionist and discursive

This categorization is generally considered a valid form of classification. For a start, the fact that a social movement leads to political or social consequences does not mean that it moves according to the aims and ideals that have been determined by these categories. What we mean here is that each movement may harbor within itself certain tendencies within these categories, continuously or for a certain period of time.

In short, these categories may facilitate analysis, but they may overlook critical inner dynamics of movements. Thus, an objective analysis has to take into consideration the inner dynamics, principles of existence, ways of expression, and types of discourses that pertain to these movements.

When we consider the efforts of Western research concerning movements in the Muslim world, we see that this approach views most of the movements as anti-colonial or anti-Western. In Muslim countries that exist under totalitarian regimes, Islamic movements, communities, and groupings exhibit a tendency to formulate broad social transformation movements, and thus are often designated as reactionary and political. However, that each tendency should carry a political or ideological aim is neither a scientific given, nor a commonly held opinion. The emerging trend of becoming more Islamic in Muslim societies is one such trend. In this trend, there is not a direct connection to politics or to reactionary mobilization. Here, however, we should point out that "forming an agenda or demand for social change" has a completely different meaning in society compared to its meaning in the discipline of sociology. That said, the tendency in the society to become more Islamic as a result of internal motives cannot be defined as ideological. This is where "Islamization" and "Islamism" differ.

In regard to the phenomenon of community, this truth must always be kept in mind. Community manifests itself as the result of a tendency that develops on its own in society. The point is not to formulate an alternative to a society's central identity (as can be observed in radical and ideological movements); rather, in its social and broad tendencies, society demonstrates its ability to express itself in different ways—sometimes as a civil organization, sometimes as a religious community, and sometimes as a political party. There can be nothing more natural than the fluctuating trends of religious tendencies and increased sensibilities in Muslim societies. This tendency manifests itself at times in the shape of organizations, and at times, as broad sweeping movements.

Some articles and studies that analyze the Gülen movement have held onto the schematic tendency to present it as an ideological movement. That is to say, they have tried to weaken its legitimacy by reading it as a reactionary formation that seeks to present an alternative social identity. This effort has turned out to be fruitless. For the Gülen movement considers social and ideological pressure as being opposed to the soul of religious communication. Religious communication addresses free will and freedom of choice, and it calls to the natural mechanisms in human nature. Upon us all, the Creator placed mechanisms that enable each conscience to recognize Him, and to let Him be recognized. This is what the community calls out to: common sense, conscience, and a healthy nature.[6]

The Gülen movement does not use imported methods of propaganda when calling out to the individual and the society. As we have pointed out many times, it has produced its own internal action method and its own dynamics for communicating the faith. It tries to render each worldly relation as spiritual and connected to eternity. All the dynamics of the movement are molded with spirituality and transcendentalism. Consequently, the relations within the movement prioritize altruism, devotion, and loyalty. It avoids promoting worldly aims, benefits, or interests. If we do not analyze a movement with its own inner dynamics and ideals and if we move with ready-made models when considering entirely new frameworks, then we will not be able to come to the right conclusion.

COMMUNITY AND SOCIALIZATION

Often, modern approaches do not consider a particular community's mode of organization as being in line with modern society. The reason for this is that they believe the ideology of modernization increases individualism. This may be true to a certain extent; however, it is not a valid consideration or approach for all kinds of social order. Those who conceive formation of communities to be against modernization—that is, those who conceive it to be a social form that existed in the pre-modern period—consider individualism in modernity as a social given. In the West, the development of a new individualism is perceived as one of the most important gains of modern philosophical thought. All sorts of ideas concerning freedom and liberty emphasize individualism.

In practice, modernization has made individuals lonelier. Individuals are being left unprotected in the face of demanding social and economic processes. This socio-psychological phenomenon has prepared the ground for the cultivation of communities that carved out a public space in the modern society for their participants. Indeed, the phenomenon of increased communities and local formations is not one that pertains solely to late modernizing societies or to societies that failed to modernize. It is a social form that is very visible in the whole of the world today.

When we take the case of the Islamic world in particular, we see that this phenomenon has deep, broad, and long sociological and historical foundations. Islam is a religion that encourages helping one another. The organization of good deeds, solidarity, and sharing is connected to the principles of social justice. Islam encourages solidarity and sharing, and paves the way for public organizations around such good deeds based upon mobilizing every believer's potential for benevolence and virtue. In Islamic history, most institutions of public service have come about as a combination of popular charity and Islamic principles of solidarity. This is why the concept called class struggle has never been an element of the Islamic history rendering class struggle analyses useless for the Muslim world.

There is a need to avoid treating the formation of communities or movements as marginal. The appearance of radical movements has more to do with the alienated sections of the society than with the formation operating within the prevailing religious or cultural framework of the society. Deep feelings of deprivation, coupled with certain feelings of being excluded from the current social identity, turn some small groupings into the catalysts of marginal organizations. While such movements might begin as mere opposition movements, they often transform into political and/or militant challenges. The active members of such organizations transmit an organizational consciousness to their members that conveys a sense of disconnection from mainstream social processes. When this radical disconnection from the general identity is coupled with a cavalier psychology that has no regard for individual lives, we can see what sort of results appear at the end.

The Gülen movement as a catalyst

Conflict and alienation are not necessarily adopted by all formations within the society. Any community or movement that has an encompassing focus has to act in conformity to the existing notions of social identity. Movement or communities that try to provide service in various sectors of the society should be differentiated from non-governmental organizations that choose a single field of effort.

The Gülen movement is an important and ideal example of such formations. As has been mentioned above, its base in the masses is not composed solely of members of the lower middle classes, people from the countryside, or those who have experienced a certain amount of deprivation or exclusion from society. Most participants share Turkey's general social identity, they are mostly educated and open to social interaction. Overall, the movement does not advocate any stance against the current political structure or the version of national identity promoted by the state.

Due to its widespread basis in the society, the Gülen movement can neither be analyzed through classical theories of modernization, nor categorized as a marginal or fundamentalist movement. It should not be forgotten that this movement aims to enrich society through innovative ways of social participation and volunteer work in the principles of positive action and adherence to the law. This makes the function of the movement critically important in terms of playing the role of a catalyst fostering habits of cooperation and mutual

respect in the society weakening the tendencies of apathy and indifference to what goes on in the society.

There is a caveat here not to attribute its mission solely to a
catalyzing religious awareness. Its willingness to move beyond the
limited scope of religious communities shows the movement's
capacity to extract from the Islamic ideals a basis of action with
broader and more humane themes. This feature of the movement
highlights its role to provide a basis of participation for all segments of the population, some of which may be affected by the
rapid modernization. It aims to protect individual identities from
fragmentation, and it provides a feeling of self-confidence in individuals with fragmented identities (as the result of social transformations) by raising the awareness of one's own identity.

CHAPTER THREE

Cultural Perspective

CULTURAL PERSPECTIVE

BASIC CHARACTERISTICS OF THE WESTERN SCIENCE AND THOUGHT

It seems useful here to delineate some basic characteristics of the Western science and its outcomes before I proceed to outline the thoughts, interpretations, and convictions of M. F. Gülen on science, reason, and scientific progress. This will help us understand his attitudes toward the Western thought as well as his mentality and thought.

Gülen has an intellectual background that relates to the Western thought since his youth. He also has a firm knowledge of philosophy, along with his religious and social grounding. Yet, as we mentioned earlier, his philosophical capacity has always been shadowed by his religious and social activities. Turkey first became acquainted with his knowledge of philosophy and intellectual capacity in the 1990s, when his views on such matters as culture, politics, state, democracy, reason and thought, moral values, tolerance, art, and philosophy were publicized in the media in the form of interviews.

The worldview of the modern Turkish people is a result of a long political and intellectual process that began with the Tanzimat Period, in 1839, when political reforms were introduced in the Ottoman state. The process led to the tradition of the *ulama* (learned men or scholars of Islamic theology) and its institutional structure being secularized following the process required by Western modernization. This, again, led the *ulama* tradition to become isolated from scientific circles. With the establishment of the new Republic (Cumhuriyet), the concept of the *ulama* transformed into to the concept of the *aydın* (intellectual). In fact, the word "*aydın*" (intellectual) is a modern secular term. It evokes an intellectual who turns his or her back to the legacy of the traditional expressions of reality and, instead, becomes oriented to the Western way of science. The process of the Westernization transformed all concepts in the traditional thought and science. *İlim–bilim, münevver–aydın, mütefekkir–entelektüel* no longer signified the same thing.[1] This transformation of thought culminated in the total separation of social and scientific knowledge from the tradition of religious thought. The secularization of philosophical and scientific thought shook the authority of the *ulama* tradition over social and scientific matters and left it in an isolated position.[2]

With this conception of the intellectual (*aydın*) and scholars of religion (*ulama*) in mind, the image of Gülen, who had a deep intellectual background—a man who was not just an ordinary *hodja* (teacher) or preacher—attracted the attention of the public. Gülen was educated not in modern institutions, but in the institutes of the *ulama* tradition. As a consequence, some secular-minded circles in Turkey regard his background in this regard as problematic and risky. The secular elite is not able to envision that a scholar of religion could be interested and well versed in the philosophical, political, social, and cultural matters of the time. They are of the opinion that science should stay in the hands of secularly oriented scholars. For them, secular intellectuals and scholars should exercise their authority in today's world, just as the *ulama* had exercised political, social, and intellectual authority in former times. Therefore, the secular elite is quite reluctant to share their monopoly over the production of knowledge. Thus Gülen has appeared and still looks an enigma to them.

This condition is, in fact, a small reflection of the separation of science and religion in the West. The conflict, or the battle between the Christianity and the circles of science in the West, ended up with the permanent partition of the two realms. As a result, religion, that is, Christianity, was reduced to a worldly phenomenon, and it was confined to the walls of the church and the individual sphere. This Western experience was rapidly transferred to other societies of the world, and it became a widespread phenomenon through the process of Westernization. The Islamic world received its share from this development when the ruling elite in the attempted to transform their societies with an ideological blindness that treated Islam in the same context with Christianity. This new atmosphere in the Muslim world damaged the *ulama* tradition and the hierarchy of Islamic thought, and the doors of scientific institutions were kept closed to those who wanted to engage in philosophical and intellectual matters with their religious identity.

Now we may proceed with the basics of the Western science. I do not aim to outline and analyze all aspects of the history of Western thought. Rather, I will deal with the scientific tradition of Western thought from three angles: rationalism and objectivity, positivism and progress, and politics of science and the state. This approach, I hope, will sufficiently outline the rules and the patterns of Western thought and science in general.

a. Rationalism and objectivity — the universalistic dimension

One of the main principles of the Western scientific view is the concept of "rationalism," which requires science to be systematically and visibly produced, and that all other traditions of science are invalid. Rationalism is accompanied by the ideology of "objectivism," and by a "quantitative interpretation of knowledge." It is assumed that scientific knowledge produced in strictly rationalist and objective methods is universal. With this declaration, a new condition is prepared and a new way is opened for this unique science to prevail. In fact, the West might theoretically allow new ways for other traditions of science to interact with their Western counterparts so that these could produce a synthesis and new scientific traditions together. Yet this has never happened because the competition is essentially organized in order for Western science to win.

This ideology has effectively eliminated non-Western science in many places. This process has been a successful one on the part of Western science—not because its counterparts were unsuccessful, but because societies that produced and adopted Western science secured a greater military power over others, as Thomas Kuhn (b. 1922), Immanuel Wallerstein (b. 1930), and Paul Feyerabend (b. 1924) purport.

We have all been indoctrinated by such principles of the Western way—rationality, infallibility, and universality. In recent times, intellectuals and thinkers from the West, such as Kuhn, Wallerstein, and Feyerabend, have shown us why this indoctrination was wrong by questioning the ways and means of rationalism.[3] According to Feyerabend, science can neither be wholly rational, nor be dependent on universal methods and systems; and despite amazing advances in the last two centuries, Western science can not unlock the mysteries of the human condition. It is neither a faultless system of knowledge, nor one which stands for the continual benefit of humankind. It has been victorious not because it is rational or self-made, but because it has had the power of the state on its side, and it has used this to eliminate other cultures and ways of science, and to declare them as being irrational and unscientific.

Furthermore, Western science concludes that scientific laws connect the world, the universe, human being, and society, and the discovery of these laws will illustrate the scientific independence of these laws in time and space. This understanding of science is very often judged in the West as a secularized version of Christian thought. It is said that this conception of science accommodated nature in place of God, for presumptions over the idea of absolute certainty were borrowed from the truths of religion, and modern materialistic rationality was developed in place of the theological approach that dominated cosmological knowledge.[4] The philosophies of nature and scientific researches produced in the early period were all interpreted as opening the way for rationalism.

In contrast, the old teleological theory always emphasized a constant relationship between God, humans, and existence—albeit not a comprehensive one. That is, though it had some deficiencies and drawbacks, the old theological approach defined the universe as being dependent on a Creator. However, the science of nature reduced this relationship to a mechanistic level, transferring the concept of a God-centered universe into rationalism, and emphasizing humans and their material relationships. Thus, the ultimate reality was determined not as the existence of God, but as reason itself; thus, human beings and their function in nature emerged from the rational laws of nature. When rationalism interpreted existence, its norm was neither transcendental nor ultimate causes, but the objective norms of reason.

b. Positivism and progress

The scientific revolutions that occurred in the West in the sixteenth and seventeenth centuries slowly led Western thought to a union with the positivistic approach of the nineteenth century, which was the rising ideology of the time. The mechanistic worldview that was developed by Galileo, Kepler, Copernicus, Newton, and Boyle was modeled according to a solid materialistic and positivistic worldview with the help of rationalism. By the nineteenth century, positivism was the primary ideology shaping Western scientific thought.

Positivism, which represents an empirical approach to the philosophy of science, is based on using observation and experimentation to interpret and explain existence. It assumes positive knowledge only, and it limits knowledge to perceptions by the human senses. It rejects other ways of knowing by placing great emphasis on the fact that knowledge can only be obtained and explained empirically.

This mechanistic view of science explains the structures, actions, and relations which exist in the laws of nature. Positivists claim that the internal order of existence is determined by innate laws, and that existence has no metaphysical, animistic, or transcendental power within itself. Thus, we may discover this internal law only by positive and empirical methods. Positivism, in short, does not ask human reason to look for ways of explanation other than empirical experience.

Positivism was applied in the fields of sociology, philosophy, and political sciences by such Western thinkers as Saint-Simon, Comte, Mach, Kierkegaard, and Sartre. With the development of the Enlightenment and theories of evolution in the nineteenth century, the ideology of progressivism had been idolized. The concepts and theories of existence, human being, nature, and society were reorganized according to the ideology of evolution. Every new discovery brought with it new solutions and opened new fields of research, thus drawing great attention to scientific knowledge. The Western view came to assume that nature also had a history of progress. This belief, along with the positivistic ideals of the Enlightenment, enforced the idea of "progress" and claimed that humans and human societies, which were parts of nature, also made progress; that this progress had laws that could be scientifically determined; and that such laws could be specified through empirical and experimental knowledge.

In his book, *The Structure of Scientific Revolutions,* T. S. Kuhn argues that science has an ideological structure in the same manner as political revolutions. According to Kuhn, scientists, philosophers, and historians have always declared their own views of science to be the highest point which humanity can reach. It is a widespread ideological attitude to embrace the outcomes of science as the only possible position one can reach. But was it really so? Did science and knowledge follow a constant and straight line? Were there not different options or alternative methods that contributed to this progress? In the 1960s, Thomas Kuhn asked these questions and struck a blow in the reign of progressivism and scientific thought.

Though Kuhn did not have such an intention in the beginning, his book, when considered together with the work of Karl Popper, made a great contribution to the transformation of the positivistic theory of science. Kuhn clearly stated that when scientific thought attempts to present a proven reality, what it presents, in fact, are certain value judgments. To him, such value judgments are not absolute and they can be transformed. A judgment that was right yesterday can be wrong today. The history of science proves that the scientific enterprise did not emerge as an uninterrupted or non-stop accumulation; it was sometimes greatly interrupted by revolutionary transformations.

There are countless scientific theses, paradigms, and ideas that conflict with one another. According to Kuhn, modern science is the result of interactions and conflicts that have occurred between different paradigms. In this regard, "progress" in the field of science cannot be measured by one particular tradition or one particular method. In addition to knowledge gained from the scientific method, society should account for historical and social conditions, religious and moral sentiments, and different value judgments and preferences. Kuhn tries to write an alternative history of science. He argues that we should conceptualize objective norms that exist independently of certain theories so that the concept of scientific progress can be made viable and comparable. Yet when one observes the history of science, one sees that great scientific enterprises that have led to progress have emerged not from the results of objective norms, but as the results of constant conceptual revolutions based on the dialectics of different approaches. Moreover, sociological and psychological factors were involved in these dialectics and conflicts. According to Kuhn, scientific knowledge cannot be separated from the beliefs and convictions of the one who produces it. When alternative views of science emerge, the production of science and scientific progress become enveloped in a power struggle.

Kuhn's criticisms have deeply shaken scientific circles in the West and the positivistic tradition in general. Kuhn was the first to question the past two-century authority enjoyed by the scientific community, and in this way, Kuhn's work was an admirable and courageous attempt to question the Western imagination. Many scholars and thinkers, like Popper, Lakatos, Althusser, Wittgenstein, Feyerabend, Duhem, and Quine, have questioned the Western way of science, each with their own arguments; none of them, however, has been as well received as Kuhn.

While questioning the Western way of science in the 1960s and 1970s may not be as significant or meaningful today as it used to be, it did leave its mark on the field of scientific inquiry. While there have been some new advances in the area of alternative approaches, Western science still attaches itself to the Newtonian mechanistic approach and to the ideology of certainty in the face of sometimes blatant contradictions. Thus, we may reach a conclusion that the West employs an ideological attitude here. And we may, therefore, declare that one cannot clearly specify the Western approach to science without specifying the relationship between knowledge and power.

c. Politics and ideology—science, power, and state

Throughout history, there has existed a strong connection between knowledge and social order. Theories of power have always been based on a domineering understanding of science. Experimental studies that empower military strategies have always relied on important branches of mathematics; for centuries, astronomy was seen as related to navigation and long-term political control of the world. Europeans used astronomy when they spread to the New World during their expansion period. And scholars and authors who were in close contact with the kings and queens of Europe began to support the reformation of knowledge not only to employ knowledge to improve the lives of people, but to use it as a weapon in the hand of the state.[5]

The most enthusiastic of these scholars was the famous English philosopher and naturalist, Francis Bacon (b. 1561). Bacon believed that science should be practiced under the full control of the state. He characterized intellectuals who favored individualism as demonic exegetes whose aim was to reach the ultimate reality directly and individually with no help from clergymen, and also to endeavor to attenuate religious enthusiasm.[6]

Francis Bacon established his thought in this regard on two fundamentals: the first was the spread of the philosophy of nature ("the science of causes"); the second was the spread of power ("the spread of the humanistic empire"). For him, knowledge was equal to power. He effectively interpreted the philosophy of nature in favor of keeping nature, human being, and society under control. While he personally defended the idea that the philosophy of nature should be extended to people, rich aristocrats and scientists such as Robert Boyle (d. 1691) adapted his idea to the social reality. In short, knowledge became increasingly manipulated to serve political, religious, and social authorities in the late European period.[7]

Increasingly, then, science became a political and ideological agent that facilitated the establishment of the centuries-long Western colonial enterprise. Feyerabend endeavors to question the philosophical fundamentals of modern science by raising such questions. He fervently claims that science was sanctified, and a church of science was almost established. For Feyerabend, the argument that science was claimed to be infallible was both baseless and not provable. Feyerabend maintains that scientists acted like the churchmen of the past, for their teachings were considered to be the ultimate knowledge, and the presumption that science is a naturally powerful entity had been made into a doctrine of faith for everyone. Moreover, science was not thought of as a partial or isolated institution; rather, it was made the basic component of democracy—just as the church had been made the basic part of society in the past. He argues that the church and state were, of course, carefully separated from one another. The state and science, however, were inseparable. In short, Feyerabend argues that science is no different than other ideologies that compete with one another for epistemological supremacy. He believes that the conditions of the nineteenth and twentieth centuries sanctified and, therefore, regarded science as a liberator or "secular messiah."[8] Ideologies can be corrupted to become dogmatic religions. The pattern of scientific progress, especially after the Second World War, is a good example in this regard. Feyerabend explains that the principles that originally gave human being the necessary ideas and power once-upon-a-time—so that he could overcome the fears and prejudices that autocratic religion had exposed to him—are now making human beings slave to their selfish interests. He warns people to be careful not to be deceived by the liberalist rhetoric of some propagandists who appear as if they observe the interests of the people. The political and sociological power of science, and the boundaries it draws, rather than having been carefully considered to provide for the greater good, were, in fact, arbitrarily dictated.[9]

d. Religion and metaphysics

Western science has also developed a view of science that is also open to a religious and metaphysical dimension. This view, however, has not been as influential. Theology and the theory of creation have always remained weak as ideological and political views made headway. In fact, many concepts and theories put forth by the majority of first-hand scientists and thinkers, which actually underline the need for the belief in God, were ignored and distorted by later scientific developments. European scientific thought was greatly open to metaphysical values in the sixteenth and seventeenth centuries. It adopted a view that stressed the point of science as being a means to find God and His attributes reflected on earth. New scientific developments in the future, of course, would force other scientists to question the negative approach developed by some scientists who were against religion. We all know that such notables as Kepler, Galileo, Newton, Boyle, Descartes, Paracelsus, and even Bacon, perceived the universe as a book emerging from the willpower of God.

Aristotelian natural philosophy had been Christianized in the culture of scholasticism. Throughout a long period of adaptation, mismatches between some pagan perspectives and Christian doctrine were annihilated, set aside, or reconciled. The institutions of Catholicism internalized traditional bodies of science, natural knowledge, and cosmology associated with Aristotle, Galen, and Ptolemy, Anselmus, and Thomas Aquinas, so much so that in Europe, these views were accepted as the only authority until the fifteenth and sixteenth centuries. The geocentric system of Ptolemy was officially recognized by Christianity until the heliocentric system of Copernicus and Galileo was introduced. Galileo's observation that the world revolved around the sun conflicted with the fundamental doctrine of Christianity that claimed the sun revolved around the earth.

Galileo did not intend to challenge religion, but to present the view that nature, emerging from the will of God, resembled the Bible as a book to be read. He maintained that biblical references to the stability of the earth and to the mobility of the sun were to be taken not as literal truths, but as metaphorical ones.

Naturalists who supported and developed the Copernican view of the universe in the sixteenth and seventeenth centuries attacked the geocentric view in various ways. Though they were committed Christian believers, they rejected the idea that the earth was the centre of the universe. They believed that it was only one of many planets revolving around the sun. All these views would bring about a conflict between science and religion. This chain of events gave grave concern to the Church despite the fact that natural philosophers were not targeting the beliefs of Christianity as they established the base of the mechanistic worldview. In fact, they emphasized that the terrific congruence in the universe was presided over by a Creator.[10]

While the mechanistic worldview was being developed, the concept of the "Book of Nature" also came into use. The Swiss Renaissance medical man, Paracelsus (d. 1541), had been perhaps the first since Saint Augustine to challenge people "to read the Book of Nature." To him, real philosophy was written in the grand book, the universe, which stands continually open to people's gaze. It is written in the language of mathematics, and its characters are triangles, circles, and other geometric figures, without which it is impossible to understand a single word of it.[11]

Then, in the 1660s, Robert Boyle (b. 1691) wrote that every page in the great volume of nature is full of hieroglyphs, where things stand for words, and their qualities for letters. Boyle defined natural scientists as natural priests, and he assigned them the task of "telling people of the existence of an omniscient and omnipotent God." In the 1670s, the French Cartesian, Nicholas Malebranche (b. 1715), said, "When I see a watch, I have a reason to conclude that there is some Intelligent Being, since it is impossible for chance and haphazard to produce, to range and position all its wheels. How then could it be possible that chance, and a confused jumble of atoms, should be capable of ranging in all men and animals such abundance of different secrets, springs, and engines, with that exactness and proportion? This clear evidence of contrivance in the natural world is one of the great motives to religious belief. And those whose natural knowledge is greatest are expected to be the most disposed to venerate God's creative wisdom." In 1961, the English naturalist John Ray (b. 1705) offered the eye of a common fly as a powerful example of God's designing intelligence and beneficence. English philosophers then came to believe that God's potency could not have been confined to nature only.[12]

The "Book of Nature" metaphor was developed in the West between the fifteenth and seventeenth centuries, and it has been a philosophical and scientific base for proving the existence of God for years. God was believed to have written two books: one was the "Holy Book," and the other was the "Book of Nature." However, scientific developments were later interpreted in a positivistic and secularist way. And once science was secularized, theories of creation suffered gravely. This brought political and societal problems that, in the end, would challenge the authority of Western science.

GÜLEN'S VIEWS ON THE WESTERN SCIENCE AND THOUGHT

Gülen's views differ from the Western thought in several ways. First, he objects to some ideological views that, he believes, penetrated Western science and colored its fundamentals. He principally criticizes the materialistic dimension of Western thought since, he maintains, Western science ignores celestial revelations and reduces sources of knowledge to materialistic phenomena and empirical knowledge. This, Gülen maintains, narrows the channels of science and cuts human being off from metaphysical knowledge. To him, Western science perceives and uses positivism, the idea of progressivism, and pure reason as an ideological tool. Gülen has written the following:

> Positivistic and materialistic theories have permanently suppressed the domain of science and thought for the last few centuries. Metaphysical ideas have been ignored while interpreting existence, the universe, worldly and heavenly phenomena, and instead the positivist approach has been employed all the time. This materialistic interpretation of the universe has pointed to just one way of thinking and it has narrowed the ways leading to reality. The West examined the universe and nature in detail, exercising an empirical method which placed great emphasis on reason, but it could not manage to develop a unity of physics and metaphysics. Thus, in the end, human beings have been taken to a position where they contradict their own selves, intellect, and soul. And this position has estranged their soul from their subjective senses.[13]

In a sense, Gülen sees the ideas of naturalism and rationalism as fundamental reasons for the depression that Western science is experiencing today. Western science is facing this problem because it established science on the basis of secularism and atheism, that is, by attempting to negate God. This process of secularization paved the way for a conflict between science and religion. Gülen describes this conflict as amounting to a destabilization of the balance between God, the universe, and the human being. The Church has not been able to keep this balance:

> The Christian representatives of the day expressed extremely spiritualistic views. They undervalued nature, scientific research, and human thought. They emphasized only the spiritual side of life, and they ignored the material side. They even endeavored to deny the material side...[14]

The more they emphasized the spiritual side of life, the more the scientists of nature had the inclination to underline the material side. This, in the end, brought about a conflict between science and religion. Gülen points out that the conflict between science and religion in history occurred in Medieval Europe only:

> One cannot see such a conflict in Ancient Greece, or Egyptian, Mesopotamian, Indian, or Chinese civilizations. There seems to be anthropological, sociological, and historical reasons for that. One sees, for example, in Sanskrit literature, that all sciences, from astronomy to astrology, and from mathematics to cosmogony, have been dealt by with a combination of religion, science, and magic. These civilizations did not fervently encouraged their members to be busy with science, but they did not present a worldview that conflicted with science either. Chinese civilization was the same. Confucianism did not cover a system of religion, but it consisted of strict moral codes. Thus, one cannot speak of a conflict between this discipline of values and science. Ancient Egyptian and Mesopotamian religions also have mythological rhetoric. Sciences in these civilizations included astronomy, cosmogony, and medicine, but they did not reach a position of fully empirical or rational science. And one cannot distinguish between science and magic.[15]

The science of Ancient Greece had its roots in ancient Egyptian and Mesopotamian science. Yet, Ancient Greece had a different sociological outlook. The above-mentioned civilizations set up states, but not like those of the Greeks. Ancient Greece had a different experience that displayed an individualistic understanding of life. This idiosyncratic character of Greek society did not allow one religious group to dominate another. In Ancient Greece, poets and thinkers represented beliefs and sacred thoughts, and all were open to new ideas and scientific research. Thus, there was no ambiance in which science and religion could conflict. Gülen also mentions the following in this regard:

> Religion was under the control of political authority in ancient times. Any act against religion was regarded as being against the state's political authority. Any act against religion coming from a thinker or a poet would surely induce serious tension and discussion in society.[16]

Thus, there used to be no sociological ground, Gülen contends, for religion and science to clash.

In Judaism as well, we see no sign of a clash between science and religion. This was true for ancient Jewish society, despite passages in the Old Testament regarding the creation of humankind, the universe, historical events, and certain personalities that contradict scientific and historical data. Gülen comments on this, considering the secularized position of Judaism as well as the historical conditions that Jewish society went through:

> The turbulent and unsettling experiences that Jewish society has endured did not produce the opportunity for science and religion to clash. Jewish people did not have the chance to found an organized nation state in history except for a short period. They have been exposed to oppression and deportation. These historical experiences have given them a strong sense of unity which other nations can rarely achieve. They have, therefore, been prepared to struggle and fight all the time.[17]

Christianity, on the other hand, experienced a different course of history. Gülen sees the time of Jesus, his apostles, and the early saints as an exceptional period. To him, the basis for the clash between science and religion in Christianity was laid right after this early period of Christianity. The first period of expansion opened the way for the frame of the teachings of Christianity to cover social and cultural life as a whole. Thus, the world of Christianity has witnessed dialectics and conflicts at various levels between science and free thought since that early period. As we stated earlier, Christianity strongly emphasizes that human being has a dual character. Catholic doctrines in particular focus on the spiritual side of human beings. They denigrate the physical dimension by regularly denouncing bodily passions and desires. In a way, this keeps the bio-psychic features of human beings under oppression. These doctrines maintain that a genuine believer should suppress and denounce this side of his or her personality because the more one suppresses this physiological side, the more freedom and humanness one achieves. Thus, Christianity propagates, in a sense, a heavenly life in this world. It frames a life model or ideal for salvation in order to save human beings from worldly struggles and, ultimately, to lead them to salvation. Humanity's existence on earth is a sinful existence, and every individual is supposed to find a way to escape this fallen world. This Christian metaphor has, since the first century of the Christian era, entailed a belief that the end of the world is, at all times, eminent. This frame of mind has led many Christian saints to explain that arguments about what the earth really was would be of no use in the hereafter.

Throughout the Middle Ages, Christianity established such an empire of spirituality in Europe that all of medieval culture and its institutions of education came under the domination of Christian dogma determined by the Catholic Church. This precipitated the clash between Christianity and science. Gülen concludes that this clash resulted from the excessive indoctrination of the beliefs of

Christianity. Western science, he maintains, progressed in revolt against this harsh indoctrination of Christianity.

This clash was invisible in the early period because the hegemony of the established Church was so strong. Yet, as Europe approached modernity, the new scientific generation overthrew the cosmological teachings of the Church. Copernicus, Kepler, Galileo, and Newton opened a new age, and a fresh wind began to blow everywhere. The representatives of Christian theology were also influenced by this process. The movement led by Luther and Calvin forced the pace against the extreme statist approach of the Church. This was the period when reforms began that opened the way for scientific progress. In the domain of religion, this movement brought to the fore demands such as the one for people to be able to pray without the intercession of the Church. These events led to a revolt against the social and political domination of the Church. According to Gülen, Western thought endeavored to soften and overcome this clash between religion and science, as Descartes and Spinoza kept the matter away from the attention of the Church. Descartes presented his famous dualist philosophy as if he wanted to make both sides happy. To him, science had a particular focus— nature. It also had a teleological dimension to it. It could reach that dimension, however, only by way of mathematics and experience. The field of religion was viewed as spirituality and also the hereafter. Thus, science and religion were viewed as separate domains with different aims and methods. There was no clash between them as long as they ran in their own lane.

Gülen maintains that "though the clash between science and religion seems to have eased temporarily, it has been raised again by such rationalized ideas coming mainly from Cartesian thinkers."[18] This clash did not, in fact, ease until the nineteenth and twentieth centuries, when modern nation states emerged. The clash stopped then because both religion and science confined themselves to their own borders.

Gülen questions the background of the clash between science and religion in Islam. Islam, to him, deals with the human in a holistic way, as a combination of mind, heart, spirit, and body. Islam is open to scientific developments and universal realities, with all its social, cultural, economic, and political institutions. Islam considers nature a book to be read, experienced, and observed in contemplation. It reveres nature as a monument due to its craftsmanship in the hand of the Creator.

The Qur'an, according to Gülen, guides science and free thought by encouraging people to study nature and the law of creation carefully (*sharia al-fitriyya*). Verses in the Qur'an—such as, *You will never find in God's way any change; you will never find in God's way any alteration* (Fatir 35:43)—point to the experimental sciences and rational knowledge. These two examples underlined early modern European science and thought. Gülen points out that the Qur'an clearly rejects scholasticism, conjecture, imitation, and convention: *When it is said to them (who follow in the footsteps of Satan), "Follow what God has sent down," they respond, "No, but we follow that (the traditions, customs, beliefs, and practices) which we found our forefathers in." What, even if their forefathers had no understanding of anything, and were not rightly guided?* (Baqara 2:170). The Qur'an rejects conventionalism and, instead, calls for research and observation. Gülen explains how Islam attaches importance to empirical knowledge, experimentation, observation, research, reasoning, and rationale by displaying such verses of the Qur'an as Al Imran 3:190, Tariq 86:5, Ya-Sin 36:40, Baqara 2:164, and Anbiya 21:30. Then, he deals with the issue of how Islamic views of empirical science and scientific thought flourished in the early period of Islam.

Much earlier than their European counterparts, Muslim thinkers and scientists succeeded in various fields of science by using empirical and rational methods as they shaped the basic characteristics of Islamic civilization.[19] Gülen concludes that the religion of Islam has no history that suggests a clash between science and religion.

Gülen criticizes the Cartesian and mechanistic views embedded in Western thought and science. The Cartesian method introduced a deterministic and mechanistic view to explain everything within the boundaries of the supposedly unswerving and unvarying rules of natural sciences. The first modernists—Copernicus, Kepler, Boyle, Pascal, Guericke, Bacon, and Descartes—despised traditional forms of knowledge and ignored the earlier experiences of humanity. Bacon said that they were going to make a fresh start—that they were going to found a new building. Descartes went further to declare that the thing called "philosophy" in earlier times had produced nothing praiseworthy.[20] But things did not go as they wished. As critics of science point out today, though Cartesians discovered nature, human being, and society anew, they neither solved the major problems of humanity nor did they manage to construct a methodology independent of the older knowledge. Gülen maintains that this scientific arrogance was nothing but an illusion:

> No period in the history of humankind witnessed so much technological and materialistic richness… Yet, no period in the history of humankind witnessed the science of the time being so alien to human being's spiritual and inner side as the science of modern times… The circles of modern science believed that old traditions, with all their values, would soon be discarded. To them, reason would enlighten everything, science would discover everything related to all existence, and such scientific disciplines as biology, physics, chemistry, and astrophysics would conquer the universe thoroughly…[21]

However, new physics, first introduced by Max Planck, developed rapidly right after the early modern period, invalidating the arguments and illusions of those who observe the universe behind steamed windows:[22]

> … And all these developments made clear that there could be an invisible side to existence. New developments today force us to find new explanations and interpretations. We should find tools of explanation other than idolized positivism and

weird rationalization. And such tools should take the heart, the spirit, and the hereafter into account . . . [23]

In another article, Gülen underlines the notion that the positivistic nature of science has not been able to offer anything for spiritual satisfaction:

> Neither the science nor the intellect of human being offered a serious explanation of the beginning and end of the universe, creation or the secrets of life. Such issues, which humankind has been occupied with since the beginning, remain the eeriest puzzle for his intellect. Today's science and man's intellect do not seem to explain extra-sensory perceptions, revelation, inspiration, intuition, dreams, extra-sensory sources of knowledge, the penetration of metaphysics into physics, miraculous occurrences, or prayers. Humanity today still seeks help and references from the explanations offered by religion . . ."[24]

One-dimensional science became so shallow that it made us alien to our own spiritual dynamics. It developed an uncontrollable technology that threatened to demolish both human being and nature:

> Positive sciences, towards the end of last century, became so spoilt that even some scholars, including Ruban Alves, Paul Feyerabend, and Rene Guenon, who are believed to be the interpreters of modern science, felt that modern science should be curbed and slapped. However, in the last quarter of the twentieth century, humanity intended to leave some earlier taboos behind and gained some success. Yet, one cannot say that old habits were left totally, because the number of those who see science and technology as the only real and infallible master and guide is still high...[25]

As we have seen, Gülen emphasizes the unidimensional character of Western science and also points to the fact that this conflict "between science and religion came about because both the Church and science approached the matter from just one perspective only."[26]

a. The relationship between science and determinism

In his words and writings on science, Gülen draws particular attention to the "cause and effect" relationship. He even attributes the fall of Islamic world in science to Muslim scholars' failure to observe this rule and the order of relationships written all over the book of nature.

Western scientific thought developed an overly deterministic view of scientific theory and practice. One of the important outcomes of this view was the materialistic interpretation that penetrated scientific thought. The more it sank into materialism, the more it turned a blind eye to metaphysics and to the sacred. This is the most fundamental feature of Western scientific thought. In other words, in the modern period, Western science took up only the "Book of Nature" and ignored the "Book of God." Yet both were metaphorically present in the Western and Islamic worlds. The Western world, therefore, remained shallow in explaining the meaning of man's existence on earth and his relationship with God. While the Muslim world, on the other hand, acted conversely; it ignored the "Book of Nature" and confined itself to the "Book of God," thereby falling behind the West in the field of science.

Gülen emphasizes this point in all his talks or writings that deal with scientific developments.[27] It is worth touching upon the deterministic understanding embedded in the Western view of science so as to understand Gülen's emphasis. The concept of determinism can be traced back to dialectical materialism as it emerged in the sixteenth and seventeenth centuries.

The importance of determinism in the history of science and philosophy can be attributed to the discovery of natural laws, and man's subsequent application of these laws to society and progress. Recently, social scientists have criticized the way determinism has been applied to man and society. Such scientists agree that the law of causality is also applicable to social phenomena to a certain extent. However, they do not agree that this law of causality necessarily negates some transcendental or external forces. They are aware that a severe deterministic view favors fatalism and leaves person with no willpower. Yet, such a view of determinism delivers no interpretation of what the metaphysical foundations of the worldly phenomena and the transcendental power might be. In the face of all these negative points about Western science, we can say that the West seems to succeed in the domain of scientific progress and revolutions; however, it ends up in negative social, political, and ideological conditions. This is because while Westerners searched and examined nature with great enthusiasm, they restrained their focus to causal relations.

Gülen recognizes that the discovery of causality has been the driving force behind scientific research and its acquirements, and he is well aware that it is a widely accepted phenomenon today. Yet, he believes that determinism has certain faults that keep people away from divine goals, and which erode the creativity of their intellect and will.

Gülen also states that the principle of causality is valid in social life, albeit not to the extent that it is in the domain of physical life. Here we see Gülen interpreting the principle of causality very practically. He does not deal with the phenomena of causality solely from the perspective of physics. Instead, he tries to make practical and social inferences. It is evident that social events repeat themselves from time to time. For this reason, Gülen contends that we can and should seek to assess future events in the light of the principle of causality:

> One is supposed to hang on to causes as driving forces. Turning a blind eye to them is nothing but determinism. The middle way means to be vigilant to hang on to reasons with no hesitation, and also to have a strong resignation not to feel oneself dependent on anything other than God. One should see the relation between cause and effect as valid, but should not give way to an extreme determinism. The furthest one can go in this regard is nothing but a middle-way determinism. I am not sure whether this is an acceptable interpretation, but

one can see in our culture that determinism has not been treated as such a concept to be totally discarded.

If compulsory determinism means that the same causes produce the same effects, we have no reason to object. If we follow this line of interpretation, we definitely accept the idea that even in the field of social life, we can see certain outcomes as interpreted in the context of the cause-and-effect relation, though we believe that determinism is not as widely observable in social life as it is in physical life. Thus, following this line of interpretation, we have to be careful about what course of action will result in what social results. This means that we have to have a plan for a safe future, a sane society, a firm state, and a solid international relationship and recognition. We might, otherwise, have to face surprises all the time.

We are not supposed to continue waiting for things to occur. All things are made ready for us in the other world, and they are transferred into this world. We have to determine clearly where we are, whether we are in life or out of life. If a society gives way to ideas such as "man is free on earth," then he will spend time the way he likes. Man will think that he is not supposed to think hard about the future; he will think the past and the future are nothing but stories. He will believe that he is supposed to enjoy and please himself as much as he can, and he will believe that no one should feel like rescuing the world on his own. This world is not worth thinking about too much . . . In such a society, making use of the physical blessings of God is counted as worship, and consequently, that society is dead. In such a society, the intelligentsia and statesmen are charged with the task of recovering people from their social malaise and leading them to higher goals by enlightening them with science. If the intelligentsia and the statesmen bemuse the society with the false ideas of daily politics; if they tell them that a change of government or change of regimes could potentially fix their core; if they do this instead of indoctrinating them with higher scientific goals such as finding the truth and thinking aright, they would only immerse the society into more problems . . . [28]

b. Religion, science, and ideology

Science and scientific activities have been used throughout history as keystones for ideological targets. Religious thoughts and principles have been occasionally used as barriers standing in the way of such targets. The experience of Christianity in the scholastic Middle Ages serves as a good example in this regard. Christianity had become a political and a cultural vehicle for the official ideology of the Empire in the Catholic Church. The official ideology had organized Christianity in order to use it for its own political ends for ages, and between the eighteenth and twentieth century, it organized science and scientific progress to make use of it in the same line. The mild clash that first began between Church and science turned out to be an ideological one that led to separation of Church and state. The state became successful in disqualifying religion, and it continued to use science as an ideological too—so much so that many scholars throughout the twentieth century often emphasized that science, which had increasingly become militarized, should urgently become independent of the state and its political and ideological goals. Such reactions by scholars are raised from time to time even today.

Gülen points out that this historical fact signifies the risks and the drawbacks we face when either religion or science is turned into an ideological tool. To him, both science and religion are tools to be used in the search for reality. Religion makes up one side while science comprises the other side. Man, on the one hand, discovers the relation between his consciousness and existence—and, on the other hand, he thinks of how he should react in the face of this reality. For the former, he seeks help from science together with religion's sources of information; while religion is the operative for the latter. Accordingly, the goal of science is to discover what reality is, while the goal of religion is to specify what man's reaction should be in the face of this reality. If science and scientific activity are used beyond the goals of scientific discovery, science becomes an ideological tool:

> If science does not have the enthusiasm and motivation to discover and analyze the basics of existence, such a science is

bound to be blind, and its findings would surely consist of contradictions. If it is sought for such unworthy ends as certain political and ideological ones, it would inevitably face some predicaments.[29]

In the past two centuries, underdeveloped countries were easily colonized with using science as an ideological tool. Many of the cultural elements in these regions were destroyed in the name of modern science. Religious, cultural, and civil assets eroded. In the hand of certain ideologies, science endeavored to assimilate everything to its own way. It also devastated natural and ecological harmony. It went so far that now, human species face extinction due to environmental pollution. The domination of science over nature was the end result of the ideology of making man into God. And this ideology, though it has cost humanity much, has been successfully implemented.

For Gülen, the use of religion as an ideological tool is also risky and errant: "Religion is a guide for man that does not lead him astray. It opens ways for science. And it offers profound perspectives for humanity to perceive the reality of existence."[30] Gülen points to an important matter here:

> Religion, which is in fact a heavenly phenomenon, may be used as an instigator of hatred and revenge by fanaticism, as science may be used as a facade by certain ideologies and movements to stand in the way of reality. This brings a representation of religion in an opposite way. What a contradiction for heavenly phenomena to be represented in just the opposite way![31]
>
> Imagine a house of science—it should, in fact, be as sacred as a temple—which is dominated, or enslaved by a philosophical movement. Science becomes a slave of a fanatical or, in fact, an ignorant ideology. Science becomes a damned thing there. If a religion is used for the interests of political or non-political cliques, the temples of that religion or religious group will become like a showroom of that clique, rather than becoming a sacred house for prayer. Such a misuse will no doubt damage the sacredness of religion.

If some members of a society uses the institutes of science as their own showroom, to use science for their own ideological ends, such institutions will soon turn out to be arenas where greed and ambition prevail. Likewise, if some members of a society accuse fellow believers who do not share their political views of being disbelievers, hypocrites, or infidels, such people will no doubt seem to be displaying a harsh religion which will give fear to the general population of that society.[32]

Gülen also expresses how people ideologize either religion or science because of their disabilities or impotencies. To him, some people use either religion or science to make up for their inadequacies or failures. Such misuses make religion and science move away from its original and sacred form. Gülen believes that such misuse can be prevented only by love of God, science, and reality. It is only through this elixir of love that man may keep himself away from such ideological and human misuses. Humanity first experienced such love through the prophets of God.[33]

Gülen, as it is clear from the excerpts quoted above, condemns those who use religion as their own showroom, and he also accuses them of causing both science and religion to deviate from their original axis.[34] Gülen specifies the goal of science and scientific studies to be the love of God and truth. Thus, he tries to open up a metaphysical channel by bringing the idea of the transcendental forward—an idea that has been alienated from science for several centuries due positivistic views of knowledge and philosophy.[35]

Concepts such as love, compassion, and affection have been left out of scientific research. By bringing both metaphysical and mystical concerns into science, Gülen clearly points to the old cosmological view that espoused the idea that the cause for the universe to exist was love and compassion. The old cosmological view—which established a constant and causal relation among man, the universe, and God—was laid aside with the emergence of modern science. Science plunged into materialistic views and was forced to be unidimensional—to ignore moral, religious, and metaphysical concerns.

c. Reason, science, and culture

Gülen touches upon the ideology of pure rationalism, a movement remnant of the nineteenth century. In his article in the periodical titled *Yeni Ümit* (New Hope) in August 1999, he tackles this point delicately. Gülen calls to keep away from the traps of materialism and rationalism, and suggests that Muslims turn toward the transcendental as they strive to renew their soul, faith, and thought. He draws attention to modern man, whose heart is already estranged from the spiritual sphere. And further, Gülen suggests to modern man that he adapt his moral compass to transcendental values through reason and contemplation.

Gülen deals with reason sensitively and simply. Inspired by both the Qur'an and the *Risale-i Nur*, Gülen explains how ultimate reason, heavenly reason, and earthly reason, together can produce knowledge that will bring the individual in contact with transcendence. His article titled, "The Two Faces of Reason and Being Reasonable" does not deal explicitly with philosophical issues, but it concludes that being reasonable means connecting thought with infinity.[36] Connecting thought with the transcendental and the infinite refers to having deep faith and engaging in profound contemplation. For Gülen, the Qur'an illustrates how one can realize unity by combining a cosmic consciousness with one's knowledge of existence. It shows us how we should use our reason, our conscience, and our heart together. The calls of the Qur'an regarding reason are always connected to the infinite:

> The Qur'an makes all of its messages open to questioning by reason, logic, and judgment. It talks, in a way, so as not to open ways for reason, sense, and consciousness to raise objections, and it also rehabilitates its followers in the name of reasonableness.[37]

Reason reaches the infinite through observing existence. The Qur'an calls man to reason and wisdom by asking him to contemplate existence. Reason is always asked to use the mechanism of rationalization in the trajectory of unity as if it were created for this purpose. The Qur'an declares the Oneness of God as reasonable, and it delineates idol worship and infidelity as unreasonable. It deals with this matter sometimes in the context of harmony—that is, in the context of connection—and sometimes by calling the believers' attention to the idol-worshippers of the time of the Prophet. The Qur'an calls for reason in regard to the ancient people who fell into the trap of idol-worshipping, and it displays vivid examples of infidelity, idol-worship, and apostasy. It clearly propounds how ancient diviners espoused a false understanding of the concept of "deity," and how people who followed them perished. Further, it describes how ancient people went astray in worshipping false gods since all occurrences in the universe call for the oneness of the deity.

In his *Risale-i Nur*, an exegesis of the Qur'an, Bediüzzaman Said Nursi also tackles the issue of reason.[38] Gülen expresses the way that he approaches the issue in the *Risale-i Nur*:

> The *Risale-i Nur* puts emphasis on reading and observing the "Book of Nature." This is, in fact, not emphasized by the *Risale-i Nur* only; rather, it is emphasized by all prophets, saints, and scholars of Islam. One may notice some variance in this emphasis, but one notices that the pattern is always the same: the earth and the sky should be observed only to find the reality that everything belongs to the Creator. Then, the soul of man will have the feeling of contentment, as the science dealing with the "Book of Nature" will offer spiritual satisfaction.[39]

This line of contemplation and reasoning has, in fact, been a legacy and method of Islamic tradition over the years. Gülen deals with this heritage of thought, which covers theological, philosophical, and mystical matters, by comprehensively and sensitively interpreting and presenting them in today's language. In his "The Two Faces of Reason and Being Reasonable" article, Gülen expounds on *Risale-i Nur*'s Twentieth Letter Second Station, Addendum to the Tenth Word, and the Resurrection topic in Twenty-ninth Word, by explaining that the path of poly-theism (i.e., giving companions or partners to God) is much more difficult and irrational than embracing theism (i.e., the one-ness of God); thus he raises the basic argument that believing in One Omnipotent God is more reasonable than believing in the one who needs partners.

Gülen points to a theistic posture through concepts of reason and rationality. He analyzes the approach of the *Risale-i Nur* as both sustaining and encouraging a rational process. The Qur'an, in fact, deals with the matter in the same way, for it does not cite the word "reason" separately; it is always cited as a functional and practical entity. Gülen also follows this pattern of thought in his analysis of the matter.[40]

When Muslims of classical Islamic thought referred to science, they spoke of the functional and practical knowledge of the Qur'an. By contrast, when a Western materialist refers to science, he or she refers to knowledge that can bring one power and give one the util-ities to control nature and manipulate individuals and societies.

The function of reason is, therefore, to use knowledge in this direction. The Western materialism made reason and knowledge independent of transcendental and sacred values. Yet, according to Qur'an, neither reason nor knowledge can be made independent of such values. Rather, they are supposed to serve transcendental and sacred values. Anything done in the name of reason and knowledge should point to the Oneness of God. If it does not, that means it has been used against the aim of creation in some way, and thus it is bound to drown in polytheism. And polytheism, according to the Qur'an, is a clearly unreasonable destination for our discoveries and reflection. In other words, if reason and knowledge are misused—if they are not used for mankind to better understand the aim of cre-ation—this will surely bring about negative ideological, theological, individual, and social consequences, as the society will begin to incline toward polytheism. The Qur'an presents, from time to time, examples of ancient societies that experienced such consequences.

Gülen deals with these examples following both the tone of the Qur'an and the perspective of the *Risale-i Nur*:

d. Revelation, reason, and experience

The objections raised by Muslim intellectuals in regards to Western science focus on the general ideological approach that consciously ignored the fact of revelation. They draw our attention to this conscious omission. Muslim scholars have determined human sources of knowledge as follows:

1. External senses (five senses)
2. Reason / intellect
3. Revelation

Western science recognized the first two as the foundations of science and because they believed revelation to be less than scientific, they ignored it as a source of knowledge. This resulted in two radical movements: positivism and rationalism. Positivism espoused sensory experience, and rationalism espoused the intellect; however, both denied other human experiences of knowledge. The followers of the two believed that anything perceived beyond the five senses and the intellect could not be accepted as sources of knowledge. These two approaches rejected all things metaphysical, and this rejection brought about radical changes in man's concepts of society, economy, history, and the universe.

Figuring out the positivistic and rationalistic signs and effects here would, of course, help us understand why Muslims placed great importance on revelation. Gülen also favors this categorization of true knowledge which has been a long-known classification in Islamic thought.[41] At the same time, however, he reinforces these three sources of knowledge with added clarification.

The fact that knowledge has sources, he explains, does not mean that people will attain that knowledge properly, and it does not mean that people will be able to put that knowledge into practical use or develop that knowledge to its full potential. In order to put knowledge attained from these sources into practice, society needs to be enthusiastic about knowledge and love science. And the method to follow is so important. The reason why Europe developed so rapidly and successfully was that the society was so enthusiastic toward knowledge. Everybody strove for discovery in the name of science. Science was not bound to the circles of aristocracy; rather, it percolated to all levels of society. Gülen speaks about the importance of research institutes and claims that universities should be supported by research centers. Otherwise, universities will not produce new findings, ideologies, and/or solutions. Instead, they will achieve little more than reifying standard patterns and reaffirming monotonous ideas. Monotonous ideas do nothing but eliminate moral parameters and respect towards science. Science and the will to research should spread throughout the society so that it can prevail. If a society does not have such a quality, that society is bound to have egoistic members. That society will become dominated by its selfish members, by the very ones who have no concern for others.[42]

The emphasis that Islam places on revelation as a separate category of knowledge makes Islam fairly distinctive from other approaches which exist in other cultures. Gülen draws attention to this point when he speaks of his understanding of science, saying that scientific endeavors should never be viewed as separate from revelation:

> It is the distinguished and transcendental feature of Prophets to read and interpret events duly and strike a balance between the reality of the universe and that of the divine. It was only the Prophets who realized the essence of reality in the universe. It was only them who apprehended the unity of the universe reflected and spread in various shapes into worldly existence. This is a miracle on their side and the Prophet Muhammad, peace be upon him, has a special place among them in this regard.

Man today still has not been able to go far in finding and interpreting the realities of the universe and metaphysical existence, though he had gone far too much in science and technology. Yet long ago, Prophets were granted divine knowledge about the nature of existence and let their people know this reality.

They did not attain this information through scientific research or individual experiences. They attained this knowledge through their ability to think and contemplate, their heart being ready for divine revelation, and their special relation with God. Through this attainment, they became conscious of the omnipotent, the omniscience, and the omnipresent God who sustains the universe. They observed the existence of the unity of the Divine Being everywhere. They became able to read and interpret the signs of the most powerful God in all particles of the universe. They staunchly declared the Oneness of God in their senses, minds, and faith.

It is hard to say that science has reached the remarkable conclusion with regard to man, the universe, and divinity, about which prophets let their people know ages ago. Science today is still like a creeping child and it changes its conclusions everyday. It regards many of its old conclusions as wrong, and it makes other mistakes as it reaches still other conclusions. Moreover, it cannot go beyond its boundaries, where it deals with limited issues. It is not wrong to state that science has produced no theory that has not been replaced by itself again. Thus, it has never been able to find reality. This statement does not aim to consider science as unimportant or to ignore scientific research. We rather consider that both science and its outcomes are important and they deserve respect. Thus we are supposed to appreciate them. What, then, we endeavor to maintain is that revelation is also a source of knowledge with regard to man, existence, and creation. And this source is available in the Books revealed to the Prophets by God, though some were distorted.[43]

Gülen often reiterates this prophetic source, which is named *habar al-rasul* (a message via a prophet) in classical Islamic literature. By doing so, he emphasizes that prophetic messages are "permanent realities." Here he does not discuss the scientific nature of

Prophetic messages, because the content of the revelation is a different issue. Gülen concentrates on the fact that principles of heavenly revelation have remained intact for centuries, whereas theories of science have been replaced. Even theories that seemed so solid have been revised many times. Yet, the principles that Prophets communicated are esteemed as permanent sources of knowledge:

> Many principles presented by modern sciences today were introduced by Prophets long before in different ways because their hearts and minds were open to revelation. No matter how far the modern laboratories and technology institutes go, the great majority of people around the world still evaluate the principles and findings of science according to the messages and interpretations of religion. They follow unhesitatingly the messages of religion regarding man, existence, and God, in particular, whereas even the newest and most solid theories and suppositions set forth in the name of science are constantly being replaced. Scientists of today question their colleagues of yesterday. Theories that seemed very solid yesterday are replaced by new ones today. Thus, the principles set forth by science come one-by-one, and they fall one-by-one. On the other hand, the principles set forth by Prophets have always been esteemed as solid. Their value has never been depreciated. They are still valuable and will remain so, as the source of their principles is God Almighty, who created and sustains existence, wrote it as a book, and organized it as a palace.
>
> The last word on man, existence, and the Creator should be given to Prophets, who had a special relation with the Almighty. They should be given the right to interpret the reality put before us or kept behind the cosmos.
>
> One of the specific missions of the Prophets was to inform people of the nature of their relation between existence and their lives and acts, as well as of their duties towards the Almighty. It was the Prophets who informed us about the nature of existence, giving the most convincing and straight answers to such fundamental questions as to where we come from and where we are going—the crucial questions on the meaning of existence.
>
> We are, therefore, supposed to look for the most reliable answers regarding the reason for our existence on earth, as well

as answers to what our guidelines should be in our journey on
earth from the messengers of God. Only then can we understand the meaning of existence and the universe, the scene
behind the curtain of outward existence. Only then can we
know the purpose of worldly existence, and only then will we
find tranquility in our mind, body, and spirit."[44]

THE BASIS OF DIALOGUE AND TOLERANCE IN GÜLEN'S WORLD

a. The synthesis of Islam and the Turkish approach

The most important values that prevailed in the twentieth century
were modernization, plurality, and individualism. Because modernity invaded personal and social life as a whole, new forms of religious, cultural, and political plurality emerged. Although modernity has been defined in different ways, no one will contest that
among its products is contemporary globalization. Ideological or
not, globalization has radically changed the nature and dynamics
of local economies, societies, modes of communication, and political organizations, and it has drastically altered the regulating fields
of law, history, geography, and government. While economic globalization rendered the world a single market, globalization is not
strictly an economic phenomenon. It has political, ideological, and
cultural dimensions. It is true that globalization has resulted in
increased wealth, technology, democratic pluralism, and production; however, such developments manifested alongside environmental degradation, increased poverty, terrorism, and weapons of
mass destruction. As knowledge, power, and technology were glo-
balized, conflict theories came into the world's agenda. Some may
consider this situation as an outcome of modernity, while others
may think of globalization as the main cause. In either case, we
have found ourselves discussing and redefining a series of concepts
like humanity and the individual; freedom of expression and faith;

political, social, and cultural tolerance; conflict or reconciliation; dialogue or fight; and so on.

Directly or indirectly, globalization has impacted Turkey on a larger scale. Concepts such as individuality, religion, and plurality engage public opinion in the Turkish democracy. Before the 1980s, ideological camps fatally shook efforts for plurality in the Turkish democracy, favoring violence instead of dialogue. Three generations before the military intervention in 1980, there were victims of such continual violence. These lost generations could not convert their diversity into richness and reconciliation. Although the traces of these ideologies are still alive, the generations of today are searching for ways to convert the atmosphere of conflict into a basis for dialogue. New generations are trying to improve plurality on the basis of tolerance and reconciliation.

As Kerem Çalışkan says, "humanity, the individual, tolerance, and reconciliation; these were the essence of Turkish culture after its meeting with Islam."[45] For Gülen, Turkish Muslims should reconstruct modernity by returning to their own roots, to the foundations laid by Ahmed Yesevi (b. 1166), Rumi (b. 1273), Yunus Emre (b. 1320), and Hacı Bektaş-ı Veli (b. 1271). I am using modernization here not in its Western ideological sense, but as contemporary dynamics, which we can use to solve our political, social, and cultural problems. Modernization reminds us of conflicts and of settling old accounts. In national representations of global conflicts, Turkey has immersed itself in the negative squalor of modernity, while at the same time, Turkish society can find hope in its special tradition of reconciliation and dialogue. The bedrock of this culture is respect for humanity; in the foundations of "Turkish Muslimness" (not Turkish Islam),[46] the roots of Sufism and tolerance are found. These terms came into existence again at the twenty-first century. Turkish Muslims have to realize their modernization by going back to their own roots and their Sufi origins:

> Whatever is the ruling system of a country—democracy is
> sanctified in today's world—the most important element is
> humankind: the problem of producing virtuous humans with
> excellent moral qualities. Philosophers of utopias, such as
> Farabi, always gave importance to a virtuous city. This is a
> mistake. Human beings come before the city, the civilization,
> the country, etc. Similarly, virtuous man has a very significant
> place in democracies. Democracies at the hands of virtuous
> people well trained in Islamic values can reach higher levels of
> perfection more easily.[47]

For long centuries, Turkish Muslims enjoyed the concepts of
reconciliation and tolerance—which together comprise the essence
of democracy—in vast territories. Islam is interpreted in these lands
in a soft and tolerant way. Ottomans treated people in all these various lands, as well as their languages, religions, and socio-cultural
lifestyles, with respect. Other Turkish states, including the Seljuks,
Ilhanids, Karahanlis before the Ottomans, also had the same policies of tolerance. In comparison to the Umayyads, the Abbasids,
and the Persian Empires, the Turks have favored and tolerated differences. In complete fidelity to the main principles of Islam, Turks
perfectly practiced intellectual dynamics like *tajdid* (renewal) and
ijtihad (legal deductions) for Islamic issues that are open to interpretation. Such flexibility allowed the Ottomans to develop a universal interpretation of Islam that was practiced for centuries. Such
an interpretation of Islam could be named "Turkish Muslimness."[48]
However, this nomenclature should not cause misunderstanding
since there is no such thing as Turkish, Iranian, or Arabic Islam as
far as the fundamentals of the religion are concerned.

When Turks controlled vast regions of the world, they developed social, political, and economic laws that were very much universal in nature. Ottoman tolerance and reconciliation was the result
of Turkish Sufism, which thrived in Anatolia. In the Turkish nation,
Sufism penetrated the social fabric of society more thoroughly than
in many other Muslim nations. From the times of Ahmed Yesevi
and Hacı Bektaş-ı Veli to modern days, the moral qualities of mod-

esty, consideration, and selflessness have been the yeast of this nation. In this sense, tolerance and dialogue best express the cultural dimensions of Islam. The most important manifestations of cultural Islam are Sufism, Sufi orders, mosque attendance, and Islamic arts.

Sufism (*tasawwuf*) is the name of a science that studies the spiritual aspects of Islam. The name, Sufism, is less relevant in relation to what the term represents; that is to say, what really matters is whether a believer practices asceticism (*zuhd*), piety (*taqwa*), and excellence in prayer (*ihsan*), and strives to increase his or her knowledge of God (*marifatullah*). These spiritual practices are inseparable from Islam. Sufi orders appeared three to four centuries after the Prophet Muhammad, peace be upon him. They functioned very positively as social institutions that provided individuals with training and education.

According to Gülen, the virtuous human being in Sufism signifies the tolerant man. He is the altruistic person who makes sacrifices for his society and for humanity in general. Based upon the Sufi dervish essence, this altruistic human model is essential to the foundations of Muslim society in Turkey. Gülen defines the contemporary Muslim identity under the direction of cultural Islam as he teaches to engage in dialogue with all humans, and he denounces violence as an alternative. In this way, his rhetoric prepares Muslims for a new identity that fuses an Islamic social identity and that of a modern human. In other words, he presents a new Islamic model that harmonizes Islamic principles with modern values.

Both in Gülen's internal interactions with Muslims and in his vision concerning the followers of different religions, his perspective is defined by an Islamic sensibility. Through his ethical sensibility on matters of Turkish modernization and his global conflict studies, Gülen is certain to prove unique on the global stage, in emphasizing dialogue between civilizations. While some question his religious identity and conceive his project to be a concentrated religious effort, Gülen's support for modern colleges, where students learn modern sciences, illustrates that his concerns transcend the religious sphere. If he were only concentrated on matters of religion, he would advocate for the development and management of Sufi lodges, not contemporary education centers, high schools, and colleges. In addition to contributing these progressive colleges, Gülen is active in inter-civilizational dialogue as a means to solve the central social and cultural problems of the modern world. If the movement of Fethullah Gülen advocated political uses for Islam, undoubtedly he and his movement would not have such a vision and mission. Gülen's project is so unique in the sense that it not only renews the Islamic identity, but it also redefines and renews Islamic action.

b. Human being, religion, and action

When we closely research the basis of Gülen's interest in dialogue and tolerance, we see that what makes him special is his interpretation of human being in the universe. Analysts, such as Elizabeth Özdalga, Nilüfer Göle, and Taha Akyol, define Gülen's worldview as "activist pietism."[49] Other analysts understand Gülen in his local format as a modern representation of traditional Islam, as produced by Ahmed Yesevi, Rumi, Yunus Emre, and Hacı Bektaş who were the signposts in the development of Islamic Sufism in Turkish history. Such analyses do not borrow foreign vocabulary to define him. They read Gülen locally in the format of the Turkish Islamic synthesis. Both groups stress his activist Sufi roots.

Gülen is uncompromisingly faithful to the essentials of Islam. However, he also reproduces the tolerant approach of early-period Turkish Sufis on Islamic issues for which there is space for new interpretations (*ijtihad*).[50] Gülen's interpretation, however, differs from the earlier examples, due to his more extensive and active-oriented vision. Yunus Emre, Rumi, and Hacı Bektaş-ı Veli practiced internal, pacifist pietism when they invited people to Sufi lodges. Naturally, their sense of tolerance and dialogue was limited to the social environment of the lodge, whereas Gülen opens up this frame to all people. His mission thus has a transforming character.

He understands this attitude as an attribute of those for whom the glad tidings are given to, "inherit the earth."[51] Furthermore, he believes that this ideal is the most basic explanation for the existence of human being on earth. On the one hand, Gülen encourages dialogue events that may help reconciliation between world cultures on the basis of good intentions; on the other hand, he seeks to transform human being—who has become an egoist in the modern era—into a character whose basic values are selfless service and devotion for humanity in general. Gülen is well aware that such a great enterprise will not succeed without organizing activated thought and the actions of human capabilities. From his very first sermon, Gülen's preaching, writing, and spiritual circles have consistently centered on this idea. Almost all his writings reflect the "hero of thought and action" as a metaphor for social engagement. Gülen contends that intellectually guided social action is the only way a person can help his or her society achieve certain goals. Thought and action should be combined with activities that will transform the individual first, so as to transform society later. This concept underlines the attempt to cultivate dialogue between religions and civilizations, which, for Gülen, is necessary to fulfill our role as the "the inheritors of the earth."

> The field of our struggle for the inheritors of the Earth can be summarized as "action and thought." In fact, the true path of existence in life goes through a potentially transforming action and thought, which is also able to transform others. In fact, every existence, from this perspective, is the product of an action and some disciplines, and its continuance also depends on that action and those disciplines.
>
> Action is the most important and necessary component of our lives. By undertaking particular responsibilities through continuous action and thinking, by facing and bearing particular difficulties almost, in a sense, by sentencing ourselves to all these, even though it may be at the expense of many things, we always have to act, to strive. If we do not act as we are, we are dragged into the waves caused by the thrust and actions of

others, and into the whirlpools of the plans and thoughts of others, and then we are forced to act on behalf of others.

Remaining aloof from action, not interfering in the things happening around us, nor being a part of the events around us, and staying indifferent to them, are like letting ourselves melt away, like ice turning into water. . . . For, in order to exist, the whole essence of the human being should be alert.

Being ourselves, uniting our wishes and desires with the wishes and desires of others, and then finding a course or direction of action for ourselves within existence as a whole, flowing as ourselves within our own course, within the general currents and movements in the universe, and preserving our own line while being integrated with the whole of existence, are the most obvious aspects of Islamic action and thought. . . . The real world of the person of action and thought, and their real happiness in it, are colored with the tones of universality and engraved within the frame of eternity.

Seen from another, better angle, action is the embracing of the whole of existence with the most sincere and heartfelt decisions, the analysis of existence and the journeying toward eternity through the corridors of creation . . .

As for thought, it is an inner action. . . . In other words, thought is the emptying of the inner being to prepare room for metaphysical experiences in the depths of the inner being. If this is the first step of thinking, then the last step is active thinking.

The underlying dynamic of our life of action and thought is our spiritual life; it is not possible for us to separate our spiritual life from our religious thoughts. Our struggle for existence was carried out by relying on the Islamic spirit and essence. . . . Again, just as our partaking of the level of heart and soul within the inner world was achieved by worship, remembrance, and thinking, so embracing the whole of creation, feeling Him in our pulse, and sensing Him in all the faculties of the mind, are again dependent on the consciousness of worship and our endeavor in reflection and remembrance. Indeed, every act of a true believer is an act of worship; their every thought is an act of self-discipline, of self-control, and of self-supervision; their every speech is a prayer, supplication, and episode of spiritual knowledge; their every observation of existence is a close study and investigation; and their relationships with others are divine compassion. To reach such a degree of spirituality or saintliness is dependent on being open to perception, logic, and reasoning, and thence, to thoughts and inspiration from the Divine. In other words, it is very difficult for a person to reach this peak, to acquire such a state, unless experience has been sieved by the filter of reason; reason has surrendered to the greatest intellect and foresight of the prophets; logic has turned completely into love; and love has evolved into love of God.[52]

From the above words, one can discern that Gülen gives clear messages, both at home and abroad, drawing a large vision of action and thinking that centers on love of humanity. From divine love to human tolerance, from experiential reason to illumination and revelational thinking, from religious life shaped by spiritual depth to global action on the scale of whole nations, this all-embracing vision compels us to engage in inter-religious and inter-civilizational dialogue, and offers us a new model for our relationships, thoughts, and actions that extends as far as it can. For Gülen, this is the foundation of the "inheritors of the earth" metaphor. This vision of tolerance and dialogue reaches far beyond the line of Rumi and Hacı Bektaş-ı Veli, to further borders and more distant lands. Gülen's sense of pietism is also open-ended; one's practicing religion, his appreciation of divine love, and his love for all of humanity, are not something for him alone. Gülen believes that such a perspective should be transported to all nations of the world as an active project. Therefore, in thought and belief, and in spirit and action, one has to be on the move, always.

When viewed through the public eye, and with universal concerns, Gülen's vision can be described as including all human and social processes. Because his model puts all kinds of ideological concerns aside and attempts to build model individual human beings. In this model, human beings are viewed as the creation of God and the inheritors of the earth. They should sacrifice their personal desires for the good of all humanity, and then they will surely realize their capacity to receive and exude divine and human love. Such a person would easily take his or her role in every relationship, as a member or leader in society. Any model of society can be realized with such individuals. The nature of such a person is to act positively in spiritual, intellectual, social, and other matters. Those who give their hearts to Gülen's ideas behave in such exemplary ways, and this is why they receive a warm welcome from almost everyone in places across the world where they are active, across the spectrum of ideological, political, religious, socio-cultural perspectives.[53] In the education institutions they set up in different countries, they also take with them the ideas of dialogue, tolerance and reconciliation.[54]

It is true that Gülen has a religious identity, but his piety is not received with resistance or considered abnormal in different socio-cultural environments. This can be explained by Gülen's emphasis on humanistic, social, ethical values that are shared by every normal human being.[55] In this regard, Gülen appears as a modern Rumi. Similar to Rumi's works that find a place among different nations, his voice inspires millions throughout the world, who have divergent backgrounds in terms of ethnicity, race, gender and religion. As he enlivens Rumi's spirit of dialogue and tolerance, world communities might show an increasing interest for the Gülen-inspired movement with a positive response.

c. The Journalists and Writers Foundation and the Abant Platform

The first call of the Gülen Movement with regard to tolerance and dialogue was made to the different ideological, ethnical, and cultural groups in Turkey. It was true that these opposing groups presented an illusion of harmony under the political authority, but deep ideological conflicts defined their recent past. Gülen movement broke this deep and worried silence by opening up an avenue of dialogue and tolerance based on mutual respect. In a short time, this invitation to dialogue resulted in the formation of the Journalists and Writers Foundation, an institution that shoulders the movement of tolerance and dialogue. With the cooperation of respected scholars, this foundation later oversaw the establishment of the Abant Platform and became an intellectual platform of discussion. Hundreds of respected intellectuals, artists, politicians, and scientists from different ethnical and ideological schools participated in this activity and researched possibilities of creating an atmosphere based on toleration and co-existence. Participants discussed issues that ranged from problems of Turkish democracy to freedom of thought and belief, from social and cultural plurality to the authority of the modern nation state. In the beginning, there was a concern as to how different ideas coming from different people would cooperate, but this concern soon diminished and the Platform adjourned emphasizing common points and common values. The Platform gave hope to people from all walks of life, who promoted different ideologies; it proved that people can find common ground.[56]

The Abant Platform was formed as a model framework to begin a dialogue on religious, cultural, and civilizational issues, and eventually attracted the participation of contributors from different countries and from different continents. It is interesting that this new development coincided with the emergence of two competing theories in social science, *the clash of civilizations* and *the end of history*. This incident increased the significance of the enterprise of dialogue and tolerance started by the Abant Platform. The Journalists and Writers Foundation prepared a series of books on how this Platform was realized under the name *Kozadan Kelebeğe* (*From Cocoon to Butterfly*). These attempts at dialogue emerged on the world agenda when Gülen made a historical visit to the Pope. Although this meeting was done without much publicity, it was considered to be a significant step in terms of building communication between two different civilizations. Undoubtedly, Gülen is not an Islamic representative of Turkey or of the Muslim world. His meeting with the Pope did not claim to have such mission. However, the atmosphere that this meeting awakened in the Catholic world gave this meeting a historical value. The movement beginning from the simple Islamic identity of

Gülen and which became an international invitation to dialogue and tolerance, exemplified the activist human potential generated by the synthesis of Turkish-Islamic Sufism. Although, with his humbleness, Gülen rejected his role in this development, no one can minimize the contribution of his Islamic identity and his action-oriented interpretation of the Sufi roots. Even in the Catholic world, his deep spiritual and ascetic lifestyle did not go unnoticed. Many Catholic priests and religious authorities admitted that they renewed themselves in awe of Gülen's wisdom, sincerity, and Sufi-inspired modesty.[57]

d. Dialogue, tolerance, and modernity

The movement of dialogue and tolerance is not an interrogation of or reaction to modernity. However, modernity has weakened the spirituality and has made human being belittled and insignificant. Modernity produced conditions that strengthened individualism and brought primacy of material motives against the interests of the society. In the end, human beings ended up separated from all that is holy, from their responsibility as inheritors of the earth, from human and ethical values, from love and self sacrifice. All great religions struggled to save people from egoism. But modernity struck a deadly blow to the human personality and to his cosmic integrity. Gülen's invitation came at the point when the flag of humanity fell to the ground in this front.

> As regards one's own world, a person who is unable to connect with or relate to the whole of existence and does not perceive a connection or relation with the universe is attached to and bound by their individual and trivial wishes and wants, they who are closed to general and universal truths are those who cleave, alienate, and exclude themselves from existence as a whole and condemn and cast themselves into the death cell of egoism.[58]

Those who sever their relationship with the universe lose the nobility of their soul, and thus their ability to transform the world.

Such people cannot be revivers, nor leaders of the earth; they do not have spiritual tension, and thus have no ability to act on that tension. "Remaining aloof from action, not interfering in the things happening around us, nor being a part of the events around us and staying indifferent to them, is like letting ourselves melt away, like ice turning into water."[59] This is as derogatory as humanity's nonexistence and misery. "For, in order to exist, the whole essence of the human being should be alert."[60]

Egoists care little for their society or for humanity in general. Their personal weights are very heavy. Such people cannot form a sincere or developing relationship with the universe. They cannot make sacrifices for society or for humanity.

Gülen defines thinking or contemplation as *internal action*. According to this definition, the ideal people should be active in both their minds and actions. Defining the parameters of a passive human being, modernity constructed a person whose personal weight lacks movement, who is an egoist. You cannot expect such people to shoulder the duty of dialogue between civilizations. Only self-sacrificing and sincere people can shoulder this responsibility, people like Rumi, Hacı Bektaş, who have tender but all-inclusive hearts. Those who come to fight or destroy should revive and discover their human foundations the moment they see such souls. The human being who has the pivotal role in Gülen's philosophy of tolerance and dialogue should always behave positively in thought and action. He or she should not act under the influence of his or her emotions; he should be constructive rather than destructive.

On the other hand such a person should be concerned for the problems of others. Plain piety, in the sense of practicing a religious life in one's corner with no concern for the outside world, is not enough. Action and discipline are necessary for making religious principles come alive. According to Gülen, only those who possess divine love can shoulder the suffering for the others. As Elizabeth Özdalga states, Gülen's model is an ascetic one.[61] There are no limits to spiritual transformation, to material self-sacrifice.

They are open to infinity. Whatever you do for the sake of humanity and for the sake of divine love is not enough. This is the epic of dedication. This is the understanding of responsibility necessitated by the idea of being the inheritor of the earth.

EDUCATION IN GENERAL

a. Revival in the spirit and in the essence

Gülen considers the problem of poor or absent education to be the most important problem of the century. In most of his writings, he directly or indirectly touches upon this important subject. When he speaks of revival, "resurrection," renewal, returning to the historical roots, and revival of our values, he refers to the education. For Gülen, the only way to overcome this great problem is by educating new generations who have completely dedicated themselves to the good of their nations, who are ready to make sacrifices, and who are motivated by both material and spiritual motives. Without educating and preparing such enlightened individuals, neither material nor a spiritual revival is possible.

For Gülen, there are certain obstacles inhibiting this revival. First, Muslims in the modern world have fallen from their spiritual and historical roots, which produced a crisis of identity. As a result of this crisis there are mounting weaknesses and cleavages in the Muslims' perception and transmission of their cultural heritage as alienated subjects.

What causes this process? Undoubtedly, this transformation occurs in the way Islam is perceived and practiced. Blind imitation of tradition and cultural heritage based on memorization rather than comprehension is the root cause behind this transformation and backwardness of the Islamic world. Education in the Muslim world forced recent generation to separate their cultural and technological lives from their historical identity, and thus their subconscious was besieged by Western influence. Blind imitation and dry memorization of tradition can be observed in the perception of Islamic values, as well as in the perception of Western civilization.

Alienation enslaved almost all intellectual, cultural and institutional fields. This was a common problem shared by peoples in all underdeveloped (or, not allowed to develop) countries. Besieged by Western civilization, the Muslim world experienced a deep identity and personality crisis, and subsequently experienced political, cultural and social transformations. Muslim societies sought solutions to recover from this devastating blow. However, they could not employ our historical-traditional sources and human-societal potential in the right direction to overcome this process. This was due to the fact that this inauspicious mental transformation caused a crack in the perceptions toward our spiritual roots and historical identity.

All said, the Islamic world had both human and social potential. Over centuries they developed a globally appreciated civilization; they possessed the holy revelation of the Qur'an, which encouraged all kinds of intellectual, spiritual, legal, and international relations; and they sit on a marvelous heritage of historically accumulated experience. But under the influence of the West, many considered their historical legacy dead and useless. They were reluctant to benefit from their cultural and historical legacy as they struggled to build their contemporary identities and organize their social and cultural lives. Most thought that the only way to achieve economic and technological development was by completely adapting to Western lifestyle and civilization. For a long time, these processes forced Muslims into a crisis, whereby they felt alienated from their culture, history, and traditions. The political elite quickly integrated their lifestyle with those of the West without much resistance. But their blind imitation of Western civilization did not enable the Islamic world to progress toward political freedom, nor did it give them any serious economic and technological advantage.

Undoubtedly, the cultural search for identity in the Islamic world continues. This inauspicious process necessitates a national revival of spiritual institutions. In the last two centuries, the Islamic world has endured various attempts at "progress," but these attempts never possessed an inclusive or continuous character. They were limited to certain political, administrative, and technological fields. The Turkish experience was not different. Although Turkey made some technological advances, these have never reached a level of enabling the nation to revive its spiritual institutions. Gülen in one of his essays touches upon this subject in general terms:

> For centuries now the Islamic world has squirmed in the vicious grasp of error and has remained unable to turn for succor in any way to its own spirit and essence. Whenever it has broken free and succeeded in taking two steps forward, it has immediately taken several steps back and lost itself in the byways. Such whimsical wandering or deliberate deviation, in which there is more harm than good and in which the harmful sweeps away the beneficial, hinders society's efforts to seek and find itself within itself and deeply disturbs the work done and the people who do it. We have seen everything in this wide world deteriorate beyond recovery and the wheels of the states and nations turn against their own selves.
>
> Therefore we believe in the necessity to investigate the Islamic world with its understanding of faith, its own acceptance and interpretation of Islam, its consciousness of the Divine, its zeal and yearning, its reason, logic, mode and system of thinking, its style of expressing and communicating itself, and its own institutions, which will make humanity acquire these attributes and skills. In this way we may direct our world to a thorough renewal in all its aspects and elements.
>
> The fundamentals of our spiritual life are religious thought and imagination. Not only have we sustained our life with these, but we have also taken action by relying on them. If we were to be parted from them, we would find ourselves a thousand years back. Religion is not only an assemblage of rituals and worship, its goals include giving meaning to humanity and the universe, becoming open to human nature in its essence and spirit, realizing the desires which go beyond this world,

and responding to the intimations of eternity in human conscience. Religion embraces the whole of individual and collective life; it intervenes in everything we have of mind, heart, and soul; it gives its tincture to all our acts according to our intentions, and imbues everything with its color.

The axis of every act of a believer is worship, every striving has a dimension of the struggle against one's carnal desires—greater jihad—and every effort is directed at the Hereafter and seeking God's pleasure. There is no separation of this world and the next in the believer's life: there are no obstructions between the mind and the heart; the believer's emotions are always united with their reason, and their inspirations are not ignored by their judgment. So, in their mental world, experience is a ladder made of light, stretching up to the mind; knowledge is a high bastion, reinforced with understanding, wisdom, and intuition. The believer is an eagle, continuously soaring to infinity on the giant wings of love; they are the embosser who embosses all existence with their stamp and mallet of intelligence on that bastion. There can be found no gap in any place in such an understanding, nor is there any neglect of humanity, either individually or collectively.

Those who perceive religion as being contradictory to science and reason are the afflicted; they are unaware of the spirit of both religion and reason. Moreover, it is absolutely fraudulent to hold religion responsible for clashes between different sections of society. Conflicts between peoples and groups of people arise from ignorance, from ambition for personal advantage and profit, or from the vested interests of particular groups, parties, or classes. Religion neither approves nor condones such qualities and ambitions. In fact, there are conflicts and clashes between some religious individuals, but this is because, even though they have the same spirit, they do not hold the same degree of belief, they cannot preserve sincerity; sometimes they cannot overcome their feelings and are defeated by them. Otherwise, virtue with faith cannot approve of nor lead to such calamities. Indeed, the only way to avoid falling into such misfortunes is to establish religion with all its institutions within our daily life so that it becomes the life-blood of society as a whole.

The Islamic community needs a resurrection; it needs a serious reform in its mental, spiritual, and intellectual faculties. To use a more positive expression, it needs to be revived, combining serious efforts to preserve the original principles of the religion with extensiveness and universality as far as permitted by the flexibility of the divine decrees, so that it meets the needs of people from all walks of life, in all places and times, and so that it embraces the whole of life.

Since the advent of Islam—and may God never cause us to be deprived of its shelter—this blessed system has opened its doors to renewals many times, and experienced many revivals. Schools of doctrine (*madhhab*) in general, certainly the great majority of them, represent new developments in the fields of jurisprudence and law; the religious Sufi orders worked on the paths to heart and soul and turned them into broad highways; schools and colleges, during the times when they functioned properly, were mostly occupied with making sense of the universe and the beings in it. As to the renewal and revival hoped for in the present time, it must be the combination of all these; it will be possible only by bringing all these together, by leaving off the outward molds for the inner core, leaving off the outward forms for the soul—that is, by turning to certainty in faith, sincerity in deeds, and God-consciousness in thought and feeling.

Quantity in acts of worship should be complete and quality should be the goal: words should be the means of the prayer and the soul and sincerity are essential; the *Sunna* should be the guide, and consciousness is a necessity. In all of these God should be the goal. The prescribed daily prayers are not a set of physical exercises of sitting up and bending down; giving alms is not giving up a small tax on one's income or goods to allay the misfortunes of some unknown people in unknown places for unknown purposes; fasting is not dieting or merely abstaining from eating or drinking; and pilgrimage, the hajj, is not traveling from one town to another to spend one's savings in a foreign currency in a different country. If all these acts are not performed within their own axis and courses and spirit, how are they different from comparable mundane activities? Concentrating on quantity in acts of worship can only be a childish game; crying out and yelling without spirit in one's petitions is for those who are looking only to exercise their vocal cords; going on pilgrimage while unaware of its essence is only an effort to comfort oneself with the title of pilgrim and some anecdotes of the journey. How can one make sense of acts of worship performed in that way?

The way not to waste away in the web of such negatives is by mobilizing to raise the "physicians of the soul and essential reality" which can fill the vacuum in us, eradicate our weaknesses, rescue us from being slaves to our body and carnal desires, and direct us to the level of the life of the heart and soul. We need physicians of the soul and reality whose hearts are open to all fields of all knowledge: perspicacity, culture, spiritual knowledge, inspirations and divine blessings, abundance and prosperity, enlightenment; from physics to metaphysics, from mathematics to ethics, from chemistry to spirituality, from astronomy to subjectivism, from fine arts to Sufism, from law to jurisprudence, from politics to special training of religious Sufi orders: journeying and initiation in Sufi terms.

We are not in need of this or that particular quality or ability, but rather the whole comprehensive mind. Just as the brain has connections and interactions with all the parts and cells of a body, from the nearest to the farthest, from the smallest to the biggest, by means of nerve fibers, so too will such a cadre of minds be connected, communicating and interacting with the atoms, molecules and particles of the nation-body. So will it reach all the units and organs that constitute society. So will its hand be in and over the vital institutions. So will it convey gently, to everyone in all walks of life, certain things from the soul and reality, which come from the past and gain more depth with the present and stretch into the future.

Such a cadre of physicians of the soul will embrace all, from the attentive and well-behaved children in school to those idling on the streets, and by conveying the messages of their soul to all of them, and by elevating them to the level of people who have knowledge, skills, and genius for the future, they will present them for the common good and benefit of society. In all student houses, hostels, schools, institutions of higher education, and places of repose, worship, and spiritual enlightenment, they will purify everyone, from all sections and levels of society, of the foulness of the age, and channel them to human perfection.

Moreover, this cadre will tame the powerful weapons of the media, such as newspapers, journals, the radio and television, and will make them the voice and breath of national and religious life, and through these media, they will teach the owners of the darkest feelings, thoughts, and voices ways to become human.

Moreover, this cadre will save our institutions of education and training, which now change their forms and directions according to internal deviations and foreign pressures, which sway with the wind from the command and control of others, and will make them instead open and responsive to the requirements of the present, re-ordering and organizing them according to historical perspectives, and raising them by use of styles, methodologies, and a high standard of planning, to be places of great quality and purpose.

Thus, in sum, we will rise from the misery of rigid and empty formalism to true scientific understanding; from dignifying diverse vile and disgraceful works with the title of "art" to true art and aesthetics; from customs, addictions, and obsessions of unknown origin to the consciousness of a morality based on history and religion; from the snares of various gnawing thoughts in our hearts to the oneness of service, submission, consciousness, as well as resignation and reliance on God.

The world experiences this rush of reformations. However, we do not believe that anything new will emerge from the tatters of capitalism, or the fantasy of communism, or the debris of socialism, or the hybrids of social democracy, or old-fashioned liberalism. The truth of the matter is that if there is a world open to a new world order, it is our world. Coming generations, looking back, will probably consider it our "Renaissance."

This revival will make our feelings and horizons of thought, and also of understanding of art and aesthetics, gain depth and variety greater than it has had until now. In this way we will find our own aesthetic pleasures, reach our own music, and discover our own romanticism. By establishing our own people on a strong foundation in every field, from science to art, from thought to morality, we will secure their future.[62]

b. *Revivification in history and future*

The sources of Gülen's philosophy about culture and education are marked with his emphatic approach to history and tradition. This approach is radically different from those who carefully barricade themselves from their history so as not to have a conscious, warm relationship with their tradition. Conceptual disputes often make isolate history and traditional inheritance to the point that it resembles a farm that dried from years of agricultural exploitation.

"Revivification in history and future," without a doubt, is as huge a topic as it actually needs a thick book just to discuss its implications. In order to fully grasp and work out the subject, we need to go through our whole intellectual and cultural history. The conceptual and theoretical analysis of the past and future constitutes a long caravan of thoughts that go far beyond the limits of this book. The reason we feel the need to touch upon this subject is that when Gülen speaks about the matters of culture and education he normally addresses an audience who already have a background of certain mentality and education to enable them grasp what he is referring to. He is not in favor of quarreling or using dialectics as a method. In his writings, essays, and talks his style and manner of argumentation are carefully isolated from dialectics. Every reader that has entered his world sees the implications he makes concerning discussions of method and mentality in the last two centuries.

From these implications we can infer that in a general way, in the Islamic world as well as in Turkey, there are two kinds of approaches to history. One focuses on traditional legacy, and the other focuses on relations with the West. The first suggests that the roots of resurrection are found only in the dynamics seen in history and tradition. The other assumes that imitating the Western world's values and lifestyles will save us without making any reference to resurrection (of our tradition). These two inclinations survive today as two different experiences. However, both inclinations represent sometimes conservative and sometimes modernist perspectives toward the past culture and toward Western civilization.

In the recent past these disputes left an exhausted intellectual legacy. After a comprehensive confrontation with the West, a tradition of two opposing intellectual spheres formed that were usually defined as being modern versus conservative, nationalist versus Westerner, graduates of madrasa versus graduates of secular schools, etc. The methods of thinking and analysis and the conceptual materials differed from each other in correlation with one's ideological affiliations. For the same problem each side produced a different solution. On the one hand, there were Westernist intellectuals who supported—and organized—a secular lifestyle under the terms Westernization, modernization, and advancement. On the other hand, there were conservatives who emphasized traditional legacy and who used concepts such as reform, renewal, and resurrection. Westernist intellectuals developed a mentality towards Islamic legacy based on reformism and rejection of heritage. In all parts of the Muslim world this pattern repeated itself.

Let us go into more explanation about the relationship between the modern intellectual with the tradition. The modern intellectual reduces tradition to modern terms, and uses information and epistemology that was not existent at that time. He does not use the traditional information system, traditional methods, or traditional experience based on that long history. Totally independent from traditional epistemology, he only uses the world of modern terms. For such a mind, the past is past, and there is no possibility and sense to carry it to the modern times. This can only be achieved by modernization and by reforming information systems. Even though this process distorts tradition, the modern intellectual does not change his attitude. Modernization and reform imply more than just an interpretation of tradition. If this interpretation does not deal with tradition in its interpretational and methodological form, it takes us to experiences that were not perceived in the past. The phenomenon of historicity originates from this approach.

There is a point that is generally overlooked: there are epistemological borders by which every tradition is engulfed. These borders define the basic characteristics of tradition, the lines of its formation as well as the forms of how it is understood, interpreted, and transmitted. Any attempt to interpret that does not take into account these borders will cause serious distortion of tradition. Modernist approaches generally do not like to be restricted by such borders. They prefer to overrun these borders by Western thought patterns and to transform the values and information systems upon which the tradition is based.

This indifference to the tradition causes even more serious problems in the handling of Islamic culture, legacy, and sources. As explained before, the Holy Qur'an is the most important manifestation of Islam, and *Sunna* transmits this final divine revelation to believers in a way to guide them how to practice it. These two sources have always influenced the individual, social, spiritual, ontological, and epistemological aspects of all Islamic societies. This is the most important characteristic of Islamic culture and what makes it different from all other cultures. Hence approaching Islamic culture and traditional legacy is not the same as approaching an ordinary cultural legacy since Islam appears to be the most essential system that justifies the existence of man on earth.

Ignoring this fact, the Westernist intellectual could not attain a real result out of his endeavor to establish a relationship with Islamic culture. The modern intellectual always followed an ideological posture towards Islamic inheritance. Hence the epistemological basis he presented was weak and fragile. The second-class activities that such intellectuals presented depended upon terms that lacked experience and practical use. The debates over the last two centuries give us an image of land exhausted out of excessive use.

The minimizing attitude of the modern intellectual towards the perception of tradition has also caused a rift in his conception of history. This is because when the Turkish modernist intellectual builds his identity he inclines towards the West, not towards his own history and past. Therefore, whenever Gülen refers to resurrection and a new Renaissance, he always emphasizes the past, tradition, and cultural legacy.[63] Gülen suggests to those who want to implant peace in the world to study the history of Muslim societies, which can feed countless positive narrations, attitudes, and inclinations in terms of living in a harmony in multicultural contexts.[64]

c. Renewal, revival, and renaissance

As we explained before, Gülen does not enter into conceptual debates about the process of Westernization. However, indirectly when he explains his views on certain concepts, he exposes the cornerstones of his projects. In most of his articles, as main topics and between the lines, he touches upon the subjects of resurrection, renewal, revival, reawakening, and the characteristics of his renaissance. We have seen some examples in the citations made above and as follows from the article "Toward Tomorrow"; even the title implies his ideas in regard to renewal and revival:

> . . . [w]e believe in the necessity to investigate the Islamic world with its understanding of faith, its own acceptance and interpretation of Islam, its consciousness of the Divine, its zeal and yearning, its reason, logic, mode and system of thinking, its style of expressing and communicating itself, and its own institutions, which will make humanity acquire these attributes and skills. In this way we may direct our world to a thorough renewal in all its aspects and elements.[65]

Whenever he mentions renewal (*tajdid*) and resurrection (*ba'su ba'dal-mawt*), Gülen begins by stating that renewal is a basic Islamic dynamic. Because he believes that without renewing and developing our Islamic understanding on issues ranging from the essentials of faith to our reflections on the cosmos, the resurrection that Muslim societies need will not be realized:

> The fundamentals of our spiritual life are religious thought and imagination. Not only have we sustained or life with these, but we have also taken action by relying on them.[66]

According to him the basis of our resurrection will be found in our religious and spiritual dynamics.

> Schools of doctrine (*madhab*) in general, certainly the great majority of them, represent new developments in the fields of jurisprudence and law; the religious Sufi orders worked on the paths to heart and soul and turned them into broad highways;

schools and colleges, during the times when they functioned properly were most occupied with making sense of the universe and the beings in it.[67]

Renewal and revival will happen in every field by "leaving off the outward molds for the inner core, leaving off the outward forms for the soul—that is, by turning to certainty in faith, sincerity in deeds, and God-consciousness in thought and feeling."[68]

In the past Muslims developed a comprehensive and deep-rooted renaissance in religious science, technology, and architecture. From natural sciences to theology, from Sufism to logic, from city planning to aesthetics, teams of geniuses appeared. They realized the renaissance of their times. Gülen states that when the basic dynamics of this renaissance is understood, it will be possible to motivate "by mobilizing all its bright minds and souls, our nation may shortly realize a second and third renaissance."[69] In his essays titled "The World We Long For" Gülen says the following:

> Starting from the recognition of the soul and essence of Islam, and by reaching toward the reinterpretation of all existence, from the boundless divine climates of Sufi path to universal metaphysics; from Islamic self-accounting and self-supervision to the vigilance, circumspection, and self-possession which make man gain lofty values; from the cities and urbanization, in which our inner world takes repose and where we can breathe, to the aesthetics which will be the property of all; from the art which embroiders the essence and reality everywhere and seeks infinity in all it embroiders to the true pleasures of aesthetics, which becomes more and more other-worldly, more and more refined and integrates with the beyond, by all these means, this nation can open a new chapter.[70]

Even though this is a real possibility Gülen emphasizes that it is not an easy process:

> For so many years, our spiritual life has to a great extent been extinguished; our religious world has become dysfunctional; the tongues of our hearts have been tied by making people forget intense, love (*ashq*) and ecstasy (*wajd*); we have perverted

all minds which read and think into a hard positivism; bigotry
has been installed in the place of firmness of character, strength
of religion, and perseverance in truth; even in asking for the
Hereafter and paradise, with a distorted mentality, petitioners
have in mind some continuation of the ordinary happiness in
this world. It is therefore impossible to open a new chapter
without ripping such misdirected, deep-rooted thoughts and
ideas out of ourselves.[71]

Gülen explains the causes of corruption and dissolution is due
to feelings of greed, laziness, desire for fame, desire for rank and
position, egotism, and worshipping the world . . . these feelings
kill any civilization in its birth bed. In opposition to these harmful
feelings, Gülen places the ideals of renunciation (*istiğna*, refuting
greed), courage, altruism, spirituality, and devotion to the divine
ends (*rabbani*) can stand against these harmful feelings. These are
the essential dynamics of the Gülen-inspired activism. In short,
Gülen searches for the roots of resurrection and renaissance in our
own past. If we do not study our past, and if we do not bring
these roots to the modern world with a renewed spiritual enthusiasm, the resurrection we are so badly in need of will not be possible. In all his essays and works, Gülen states that only a large
group that possesses the above characteristics could ever achieve
this resurrection. Through these voluntary laborers in education,
we can catch a new resurrection and realize a new renaissance.

However, in debates and projects throughout the last two centuries, there has been an unspoken consensus that our revival and
renaissance could only be achieved by a limited number of intellectuals and elite circles. This is one of the essential points on which
Gülen disagrees with others. He believes that resurrection can be
achieved by a large group of educators, through their work as selfless spirits. This explains why he always emphasizes the significance of education and insists on the necessity of unselfish and
faithful teachers.

Undoubtedly, Gülen's intellectual and conceptual world is embellished with a style, content, and profundity particular to himself. Therefore, let us ponder on the concepts of renewal (*tecdid*), reform[72] (*ıslah*), imitation (*taklit*), and conventionalism (*şablonculuk*).

These concepts occupied the agenda of early Islamic legal schools, as well as theological, political, and philosophical currents. Questioning sources did not first start with Westernization. This process continued through Islamic history among individuals and groups. Therefore, these concepts possess rich historical and intellectual depth. Naturally, we will not enter into a long intellectual and conceptual discussion about the past and future of these concepts. We will only make some general remarks about the causes of intellectual misunderstanding.

The problem in the contemporary use of these terms is twofold. First, we must ask ourselves, "How do we revive tradition?" Second, "How do we recover from backwardness and move toward advancement." Undoubtedly, factors that triggered intellectual activity concerning traditional heritage and essential sources, in the second, third, or fifth centuries following the advent of Islam, were far different than the contemporary issues, like "civilization, modernity, and advancement," that we face today. Nonetheless, the social and socio-cultural problems of change defined all intellectual activities of the time. As new lands opened to Islam, Muslims came into contact with foreign civilizations under circumstances such as war and peace, political and cultural embassies, and trade. These confrontations caused changes in the social, cultural, and religious aspects of the Islamic world. Confrontation and social change deeply affected Islamic intellectual activities. Thus, debates in regards to the Islamic cultural heritage are a legacy of activities throughout history.

These debates aimed to differentiate the invariable (*ahqam al-thabita*) and variable aspects (*ahqam al-mutahawila*) of Islam in a general sense. This effort represented intellectual activities under the banner of revival, reform, and renewal on the one hand, while on the other, showing the capacity of Islamic tradition to survive under changing conditions. We stated before that the most central manifestation of Islamic culture is the Holy Qur'an, the Divine revelation. Indirectly, this means that divine revelation contains eternal realities (that are unchangeable). Hence, every movement directed toward Islamic cultural heritage—whether it takes renewal and revival, or reform, resurrection, and renaissance—should be in line with the spirit of these unchangeable realities. In other words, in classical Islamic culture, it is obligatory for every activity of interpretation (*ijtihad*) to follow the principles and methodology over which a scholarly consensus has been attained over centuries with regard to perceiving, understanding and practicing the Islamic doctrine. Every effort toward renewal, resurrection, or reform is, in a sense, a new construction, a reproduction of the past and cultural legacy in a new social and political conjunction. This is a human activity, and it should be in accordance with the spirit of divine revelation. As a human endeavor, this cannot be classified only as a matter of change. It is also an activity of searching for reality. It should be directed toward understanding divine intention, the pleasure of God, and His Will. Although this attitude seems to be overly cautious, it is necessary to observe the boundaries of the above-mentioned search and direction, since it directs human's voyage to eternity. Invariables stand for essentials of Islamic belief/doctrine and its normative structure, and they are perfectly rooted in Islam.

Despite the presence of invariables in the Islamic cultural legacy, Islam has the potential for renewal, reform, and resurrection. There were always necessities in cultural and social life that forced change and renewal. Any Islamic renewal that emerged within the doctrinal, legal, and epistemological framework has always revived personal and social life. Just as in the past, comprehensive renewal and revivification movements can be repeated today, and a new manifesto of Islamic revival can be initiated—on the condition that the spirit of the divine text is not abused. Such an activity, however, requires comprehensive intellectual perfection and depth. We should discriminate intellectual activities intended for the enlargement of Islamic culture from reform activities affecting the essential sources of the Islamic heritage. Reformation directed toward Islamic essentials is a slippery domain because reform is not directly equal to renewal and revival (*tajdid*, *ihya*, and *islah*).[73]

Tajdid, *ihya*, and *islah* are not more than activities that originates from within the tradition. They should stay within the boundaries of basic Islamic texts and method. Reform, too, is a call for renewal; however, it envisages a change which replaces the building blocks of the tradition and the essential discipline of needs. *Tajdid* does not feel obliged to explain itself because it refers only to renewal from inside; reform, on the other hand, has to explain itself to the masses. Because it has no relation with the tradition, neither at the intellectual level nor on the basis of collective inherent references, it has to resort to evidence from outside tradition in order to legalize itself. Between reform and tradition, there is an epistemological and ontological incompatibility and gap. Reform has an ideological nature, rather than an epistemological or methodological nature. The Reformation first appeared in the history as the end result of a long period during which the essential sources of Christianity went through alterations. The Reformation, in its context, aimed to discriminate truth from falsehood in the Christian tradition. Christian Reform and renaissance started as a movement that questioned the sources and dogma of Christianity. This movement later expanded to other fields. This never happened in Islam. Islam today is present with its authentic sources and the traditions of fourteen centuries. Reformation could not attain success without touching upon the dogmas and essentials of the official discourse of the Church, which had sovereignty over thoughts, ideas, and scientific truths. As far as Islam is concerned, the same activity is equal to a distortion of uncontaminated sources. Hence, reformation is an antidote for Christianity, but it turns out to be poison for Islam. Therefore, as for Islam and its fundamental sources, we can only speak about renewal (*tajdid*). As often repeated, *tajdid* is an endeavor to enlarge the commentary on religious texts from the inside. Although the cultural legacy of Islam has elements affected by relations of power, authority, and ideology across a long history, Islamic methodology kept the essential values of Islam intact. Hence, Muslim thinkers, jurists, and renewers (*mujaddid*) spoke of renewal and new interpretation rather than reformation. However, they always approached reform with caution.

Undoubtedly, this analysis and conceptual perspective does not give a sufficient depth and framework to Islamic law, theology, and methodology. The language and style I use in this issue is that of social sciences. Such matters have been dealt with more precisely and with greater detail in Islamic literature, with its more comprehensive terminology and epistemological borders. My aim here is only to direct the attention of the readers to the social aspects of the phenomenon. Some concepts used for certain social and cultural issues are nourished in Islamic methodology (*usul*) from a deeper background than they are in the social sciences.

When Gülen speaks about renewal, revival, change, and resurrection, he uses contemporary language, while pointing to their Islamic methodological content and background. Although he is aware of historical and conceptual debates, when he speaks about resurrection as a nation, he does not enter into such debates. This is felt in the sensitivity he shows when choosing words, and in his cautious style. He also believes that the elements of our resurrection as a nation are hidden in our cultural legacy. If this cultural legacy is studied and reinterpreted in depth, in accordance with the necessities our times, so that solutions to modern problems will be found in the long or short term—and if these solutions are put into practice with patience, according to comprehensive master plans—then we can speak of a possibility of resurrection. Gülen consistently calls our attention to the fact that, above all, there is a need for a group of people who will selflessly serve their nation and their religion. Without first educating such a group of selfless people, devoted to serving humanity, no cultural legacy alone can provide the means for resurrection. Only such a generation will transmit our resurrection to the masses. This is why he does not enter into long discussions on such magical concepts; rather, he emphasizes the need to raise such a generation.[74]

d. History in Gülen's thought

Gülen's interpretation of history and the Ottoman past indicates that he has a different perspective. In interviews conducted in the 1990s, he did not enter into a detailed analysis of his historical viewpoint. He, rather, presented an important perspective as far as his philosophy of history was concerned, in simple, short sentences. Gülen explained that he does not consider history to be merely something that has passed. For Gülen, history is more than that which shaped our identity; that is, it cannot be limited only to what has been done. The philosophy of history should also deal with the overall objectives and the imagination of historical figures that made their mark. He looks into historical events from the perspective of a representative individual who had a leading role in that event. As an example, let us have a look at the conquest of Istanbul by Fatih (Sultan Mehmet II). This was not an ordinary event in history; it closed one age and opened a new one. The opening of Istanbul was a great success, a product of exemplary thinking and enterprise. Gülen looks into the imagination of the hero at this opening. For him, what made Fatih a great man was not the conquest of Istanbul, but the vision he displayed as a leader. His endeavor was not limited to the city walls of Istanbul, which, from our contemporary perspective, was akin to conquering a village. Fatih Sultan Mehmet II's vision reached further than this, and in comparison to what he dreamed, the things he accomplished were insignificant:

> For those who submitted their hearts to the ideals of the Prophet, the opening of Istanbul is as insignificant as the conquest of a little village. Fatih was great in his ideals, not with

the things he did. We should judge his greatness with the ideals bared in his mind. His dreams were not mere utopia. If we look at what he achieved, we can easily understand that he would have his dreams come true if God had given him a longer life. We look at Fatih's dreams and, therefore, we greatly appreciate him.[75]

The philosophy of history deals with what falls in the objective domain—i.e., events that took place and that exist in history. From this perspective, Gülen's approach could be classified as subjective. In this way, he highlights the hidden reality in subjective history. He objects the trend to reduce history to events, intellectual activities, and objective phenomena only:

> Objective elements seem to be prevalent in history. However—I will tell you a different thing—objective principles grow and develop in the bosom of the subjects, like an enigma that is born out of a paradigm. In particular, they are born in the imagination of people who can develop such ideas and systematize them. In other words, historical thinking and historicity take their first steps in the form of imagination (*tahayyul*). It reaches its childhood in the form of description (*tasawwur*). Through reasoning (*taaqqul*), it reaches its youth. When put into practice, it becomes a plan or project, and it is now in its state of maturity. Hence, we should not narrow down incidents by reducing them to mere objective facts. Although it looks different, this way of thinking is relevant with historical events in the sense that it points to where they originate from and where they lead to.[76]

Gülen underlines the necessity of reading history not only by looking into what has been realized, but by also taking into consideration the thoughts and ideals of historical figures which did not have the opportunity to come to the surface. In this way, history will become vibrant and more informative.

Gülen continuously stresses the meanings of yesterday, today, and tomorrow. For him, the past is a spring, today is a river, and tomorrow is an ocean. For him, yesterday is a source of messages for humanity:

It is not that we do not judge the present by looking into the past and future. The past is an important spring, and the present is its river, and the future is an endless ocean. All these should be evaluated in the most lucrative way in their own perspectives. We cannot think like some materialists. For example, Omar Hayyam states:

> Do not cry for yesterday in vain,
> Do not praise tomorrow in vain:
> The past and the future are all tales—
> Only think of your pleasure,
> Do not spoil your life.

This is a state of contraction akin to entering a cage. The generations of today have managed to smash this cage, and even the materialist people have realized that the present situation is not satisfactory for humanity. Hence, some of them take refuge in the past, and some in the future. Those who can think deeper do not see the past as a grave. The past is the capital of our ancestors. The present is the offshoot of the spirit and meaning of the past, and it is respectful of the dynamics of history. This respect is not theoretical. We give the past its due values and want to protect it. We do not put it into the museum of ethnography. Rather, we consider the past as a living body that speaks for us, thinks for us, and whispers words to us. We see a world that speaks through streams, rivers, seas, hills, and plateaus. In reality, the future is a world where opportunities come one after another.[77]

EDUCATION AND SCHOOLING

a. The madrasa *(religious school) vs. the*
maktab *(secular school)*

Gülen is an activist who was raised in *madrasa*s (religious schools). He first experienced the basic knowledge of life, reason, belief, and action there. Indeed, for centuries, the *madrasa* was an institution that constructed the intellectual, political, and legal foundations of the Ottoman Empire. Its prominence in the rise of the Ottomans and Turkic-Islamic civilization cannot be downgraded. The *madra-*

sa was the most fundamental institution that shaped the Ottoman mindset, identity, source of knowledge, and worldview, as well as its official and social organizational types. Until the Tanzimat, it was a kind of living organism that nurtured Ottoman thinking, the education system, and social life.

*Madrasa*s were independent educational institutions that were not subject to state inspection. All of them were undertaken by various foundations (*waqfs*). Ottoman society was socially cohesive. Rich families were to endow their entities for the good of society, without considering any interest other than religious and moral sentiments. Nevertheless, beginning in seventeenth century, the social and economic order of the state began to decline, which paved the way for the decay of the *waqf* institution, and subsequently of the *madrasa* education and training system.

Since the *madrasa* was an independent institution free of state inspection and intervention, it was shaped by the dominant social and religious characteristics. That was why it was strong when the Ottoman society appeared healthy and vibrant. Society was stable because the state was powerful. Another important reason of social stability was religious and moral cohesiveness. As time passed, however, external and internal factors led to the decline of the Ottomans, and social bonds weakened. This social change caused the *waqfs* to destabilize. Because of economic and political instability, rich families no longer felt safe or secure. Therefore, they either did not donate their wealth or they began to form their own special foundations. In time, these families converted their foundations into a form from which they earned their living. Hence, foundations failed to retain their religious and social status. Family foundations became one of the factors that uprooted the *madrasa* system, as privileged classes and staff became more dominant in the *madrasa*s. Foundation trustees began to appoint incapable people as managers and teachers, and *madrasa*s were transformed from a center of learning where science was produced, to a place where merely the history of science was taught without analytical thinking; thus, old information was repeated. Eventually, politics penetrated the *madrasa* system, and it deprived the *madrasa* of its independence as an institution. While independent, the *madrasa* had reached its climax in terms of religious, social, and cultural influence.[78]

Of course, there are other cultural, social, and cultural reasons that led to the collapse of the *madrasa*. Other factors included the emergence of European countries as superpowers, and the power of westernization movements influencing state policy during the Tanzimat period. This was the result of such movements importing and substituting a Western mind-set, and a goal to change social and socio-cultural life. Such developments necessitated that the *madrasa* and educational system be re-examined.

During the declining periods of Ottoman government, the education and training systems were not unified. There were two types of school systems:

1. Muslim schools (*sibyan maktab*s, *madrasa*s, various military schools, Enderun, etc.)
2. Non-Muslim schools (schools of Bulgarian, Greek, Armenian, Jewish, Serbian, and other communities).

These schools differed from each other with respect to their methodology, educational philosophy, and religio-political beliefs. Hence, they did not pursue a uniting policy in Ottoman society. We can also argue that schools opened by foreign missions further weakened the unity of Ottoman-Turkish education system, as they became political clubs that operated against the Ottoman state in the aftermath of the Tanzimat reforms. The political, military, and social impact—sometimes to the extent of colonization—of France, Britain, and Germany over the Ottoman state was only possible because of the emergence of these new schools and the locals educated therein. As the Empire was coming close to its end, foreign schools almost equaled a form of cultural imperialism.

Now, let us briefly examine our subject from the standpoint of the main actors during the Tanzimat period, the period that ushered in a new education and training system. The main actors of the Tanzimat period were aware of the disintegrated structure of the Ottoman educational system. They wanted to unite it by employing a secular, liberal, and modern project. They thought that the disintegration of the educational system was causing social disorder and diffusion and, inspired by Western cultural and political values, they dreamed of constructing a new society. Their plan was to change and reform the *madrasa-maktab* system, which they thought would ensure the political and social harmony of Ottoman society. Their plan was indispensable in relation to social unity and Westernization projects. While the new *maktab* system during the Tanzimat succeeded, the community school projects failed. New education reform created a tremendous duality in Ottoman educational culture, that is, a period of "*madrasa* versus *maktab*." First, Tanzimat reforms privileged foreigners in the development of both religious and secular schools within the Ottoman Empire. Because the leaders of the Tanzimat were confused, they did not foresee the eventual effects this new mentality. These actors did not absorb Western values, nor did they adapt them into their social projects. They merely imitated the West, and because they acted in true appreciation of their own society, they could not establish a coherent educational and social system. The secular *maktab* was separated from the *madrasa*, and the infrastructural and fiscal expenses of the new *maktab*s carried a heavy burden.

The duality and competition between the *madrasa* and the *maktab* divided the Turkish intelligentsia and politicians, and it led them to engage in ruthless struggles that eventually led to the utter defeat of the *madrasa* system in favor of a *maktab* system that was by and large an imitation of the educational systems of the West. This struggle lasted until 1924, when the Republic enacted the law of educational unification (Tevhid-i Tedrisat). In the Republican era, the number of schools increased along with the level of literacy, yet the extent of progress was not the same in terms of quantity.

The intellectual confusion that plagued the Tanzimat elites led to the dilemma of the *"madrasa* versus *maktab"* situation, as these elites fell victim to a poorly executed vision of higher education in the modern world. Strangely enough, the Tanzimat Declaration (1839), exaggerated by its elites, did not contain detailed provisions about learning and education. Although all of its articles carried political and social reforms, the declaration, considered as a turning point for the Empire, did not include a policy of basic educational reforms. Islahat Decrees (1856) touched upon the education system slightly. But before the Tanzimat education system was embodied in the *madrasas*, it was monopolized by the state under both the Tanzimat and the Republic.

b. The madrasa and change

The social impact of the *madrasa* was broader than that of both the *maktab* and the modern school. Throughout long centuries, it helped create relatively harmonious relations with the family, the neighborhood, and society. Although Tanzimat elites wished to construct a modern Westernized society via education, the *maktab* system accomplished little more than creating a duality between social and educational systems.

The *madrasa* provided a comprehensive worldview for the society, as it integrated social, religious and cultural training. But the *madrasa* failed to recognize the change in the social and economic environment of the time. This change was exacerbated during the Tanzimat, when Western forms of life dominated the education system, daily life, and social manners, and when it crept into both the private and the public spheres of the Empire, causing every social and individual relationship to change. The *madrasa*'s social circle was constant; however, it could not provide an alternative social organization or lifestyle for a society that was already exposed to an imaginary mental change. Its conceptions of life could not cope with the reality of society, and it could not produce solutions to mounting social problems. Its social and cultural mobility was also weakened. This was compounded by the fact that much of the society was eager to detach itself from its own history, from its social roots; it wanted to integrate with Western life and styles. Thus, the society experienced a form of alienation from the *madrasa*'s firm and self-respecting educational identity.

Madrasa education digressed, while the operational and instructional logic developed in the West surpassed the *madrasa* model in every field, from information techniques to industrial and military technology. The *madrasa* froze in its formal logic and left no space for renovation or improvements. Lots of useless information was memorized; minds were exhausted by knowledge and theories that were no longer practical or applicable to daily life. Looking back to that period, the discussion is no longer meaningful for us. The *madrasa* and *maktab* have lost their socio-cultural legitimacy. Nevertheless, it is important to observe the historical and social foundations of the *madrasa* so as to analyze the nature of a *madrasa*-based scholar and activist.

c. *Gülen from* madrasa *to "college"*[79]

Gülen is one of the last representatives of the *madrasa* system. That said, he has not confined himself to the social, scientific, and mental limits of the *madrasa*. He has studied the hierarchy of sciences and social life in contemporary modern Western civilization, and thus, in addition to his expertise on religious sciences, he possesses a vast knowledge in humanities, and social and natural sciences.

Gülen succinctly expressed his ideas regarding education and its adventure from *madrasa* to college in interviews that took place in the 1990s.[80] In these interviews, Gülen made broad and analytical criticisms of the *madrasa*. He specified a number of issues and problems that plagued the system in its latter days, such as the way basic Islamic sciences were studied, the insufficiency of its curriculum, its repetitive structure, and how the tradition of commentary and interpretation (*hashiya* and *sharh*) transformed into a form upon which any kind of innovation was reacted to. He compares classical studies in the *madrasa* to the natural and mathematical sciences that later emerged in the West. Although he stresses many problems, he relates the decline of *madrasa* to the keeping of natural sciences out of the agenda. He contends that classical disciplines, such as dictionary studies (*lugat*), rhetoric (*belagat*), logic (*mantık*), philosophical theology (*kelam*), Qur'anic commentary (*tefsir*), jurisprudence (*fıkıh*), and legal theory and methodology (*usul*), were all studied in a systematic way that eventually left no space for theoretical or practical improvements/reforms. To him, this separation of religious sciences from the natural sciences was the sole reason for stagnation of the *madrasa* system:

> This separation dated earlier, back to the Nizamiya Madrasa. Therefore, some scholars partly throw the blame on Imam Ghazali. His struggle with philosophy was misconceived, since philosophy and the sciences based on research were not separated yet. Natural sciences and the sciences acquired with rationalism were negatively affected from his reaction to philosophy. Imam Ghazali mounted a reaction toward theoretical philosophic arguments that caused a tremendous destruction in the Islamic world at that time. However, his reaction was misunderstood and taken as an attitude against positive sciences. Those who opposed natural sciences took advantage of this attitude and strengthened their positions.[81]

Referring to rhetoric and logic books deemed as fixtures in the *madrasa* curriculum, Gülen argues that those books were regarded only as dialectical components of systematic and disciplined thinking about entity and property, and that they alienated the education system from social and mental life:

> I do not fully understand the late madrasa system of studying certain things in the name of rhetorical principles and what they are good for. I am still puzzled by fancy things in Arab literature. We studied the logic of Aristotle and Shamsiya with the same rationale. We were offered lots of things. Perhaps,

they were useful in terms of providing materials for dialectic reasoning, but not to construct a modern line of thought - lest they do not mean anything in the name of Islamic sciences. I early noticed that the *madrasa* did not have a modern line of rationale, a mathematical foundation, or at least a root in Baconian logic.[82]

For Gülen, the separation of religious thinking from the natural sciences ran against the Qur'an, for the Qur'an clearly recommends the marriage of religious and natural sciences. When this marriage disintegrated, an ominous process began: first, religion and science became separate within the human being/student; then, there emerged a clash between the *madrasa* and *maktab* in the education system and in social life. All other social and historical factors could be reduced to variants or products of this separation:

> In Ottoman history, we observe the Kadizadeler, for instance. They removed everything from education that was not considered to be part of the religious sciences. Thus, the *madrasa* estranged the natural sciences and research, despite injunctions in the Qur'an and the *Sunna*. Sections that discuss heavens and the earth—in other words, the *afaq* (exoteric) and *anfus* (esoteric), as perfectly put—composes nearly a third of the Qur'an. Some are discussed digressively, and some are connected to worshipping and praying. The moon, the sun, the stars, celestial systems, and the sky . . . Within the approach of Bediüzzaman Said Nursi, the Qur'an satisfies poetic inspirations as well as rational thinking and researchers. Nevertheless, the *madrasa* closed its doors to these statements. While God says, "We will show them Our manifest signs in the horizons of the universe and within their own selves" (Fussilat 41:53), we hardly saw research, examinations, and engagements with the nature of things. Although the Qur'an was read, the book of nature was left to the side. Nobody cared that both books should be taken as the basis of natural sciences, like physics, chemistry, mathematics, and astrophysics. Reading things and events in the universe is just like reading a book, and it consists of half of the obligations of a believer . . .
> . . . When the marriage (of religious sciences and positive sciences) disintegrated, both the *maktab* and the *madrasa* went

to different places. A clash emerged in the society, and the mind separated from the heart. Consequently, the book of the Universe was put in one place, and the book of the Qur'an was put in another.[83]

When we trace Gülen's critical view of the classical *madrasa* system from the perspective of religious sciences versus positive sciences, we can better understand his project in college education. Even these short excerpts illustrate why and how he links contemporary education, religious sciences, and positive sciences into a living and practical frame. Gülen's college education system paved a way for a new era, remarrying the contemporary education system, whose preference is toward secular or pure science, and the classical *madrasa* system, whose preference is toward religion. Having said that, we do not suggest that he applies an eclectic system randomly, mixing religious sciences and natural sciences. As a matter of fact, his idea of college education does not contain a religious dimension. However, it also sees no confrontation or dialectical clash between the natural sciences and values, be they religious, ethical, social, or individual. We have experienced how those kinds of clashes can ruin a personality, and a social structure. Gülen marries the mind and the heart by focusing on a concern that considers how knowledge and education should be integrated with people and social life, rather than something addressing only the brain, an external, lifeless object. In this sense, knowledge is wisdom and love. He calls this the "culture of the heart and conscience":

> One of the prominent factors that differentiates nations from others is their culture. The cuisine, code of behavior at certain occasions, traditions, and even the design of the home, take shape by recurrence and reproduction, and they become a distinguishing quality of a nation. Likewise, the heart takes shape by recurrence and repetition and reaches a level to become aware of spiritual realities, divinity, and the relation with God and with entities beyond the material world. In this regard, I think it is appropriate to call knowledge a "heart culture"...

Wisdom, a source of abstract knowledge, will transform into love. Because if one believes something and knows it to the same extent, he or she cannot help but love it. Love is relatively open to everyone, yet those with consciousness and a tender heart can easily upgrade it to the level of divine love.84

Humankind is not made up of the heart and conscience only. Education should target the material dimension of humanity as much as it targets the heart in order to reach unity:

> This is not a matter of the heart only. Surely, the heart is important; yet, one should not neglect the body so as not to neglect the world. In fact, the human being is a microcosm of the world, and the world a reflection of the human being. Saying, "You suppose yourself a little thing, but . . .," Ali, may God be pleased with him, states this fact. The human being is not a mechanism of the heart, spirit, or conscience. And he or she is not wholly a mechanism of *nafs*, the carnal self, either. Humans should be analyzed comprehensively. Different faculties of humans are subject to sole considerations. The human being, with his spirit, feeling and cognition, is a whole universe. I think that one of the ultimate stations of Sufism (*tasawwuf*) is *jam* (union). Even greater is *jam al-jam* (union in the union), through which a human being reaches the climax of secrets regarding the self.85

THE CONTRIBUTION TO THE TURKISH EDUCATION SYSTEM

The private high schools established upon Fethullah Gülen's encouragement became important in two respects: first, in terms of their social aspect; and second, in terms of the quality of education. They greatly enhanced interest in education everywhere, in circles that supported or criticized them. In a sense, these colleges contributed to spreading education to non-governmental organizations and made education the possession of larger segments of society. As the success stories realized by these schools started to receive broad coverage and public attention, people were compelled to show great interest in educational projects. Turkey was new to such an emphasis on education, having never experienced such an event in its history. Today, special education programs in the media, and special features on the news, which regard education have become ordinary practice. Now, many people from all kinds of ideological backgrounds, professionals or amateurs in this field, open colleges in an organized manner. Education is a growing field in the private sector that gains importance with each passing day. And it has been the schools attributed to the Gülen movement and their successes that have triggered these developments.

In addition to all of this, these schools have ushered in a notion of selfless service to education. Education is a long-lasting marathon. It requires serious effort and hard work. The success of these schools is based on altruism and idealism. Thousands of people serve in these institutions with unabated enthusiasm. They act with a sense of contentment, and they illustrate the idea of a soul dedicated to humanity. This is the attitude that the Turkish education system forgot long ago. Of course, there are altruistic and faithful people everywhere. However, it has been nearly impossible to attract teachers to regions of deprivation. In some regions, the application of double salaries has been established as an economic incentive. Despite such a generous offer, teachers prefer to work in big cities where modern consumption habits are more easily satisfied. Since teachers who want to work for public schools start their career in a district selected by the Ministry of Education according to priorities, the issue of appointments and placements has been the most complicated, controversial and speculative agenda for Turkey. But there is no such a problem in schools associated with Gülen. A harmonious framework of employment and teaching environment is what signifies these schools. The teachers go to the most remote corners of the world, some that are plagued by deprivation. Among these are regions where military conflict with separatist groups is an ongoing reality. Despite these facts, however, the teachers appointed to these dangerous regions head there with an utter sense of acceptance and assurance of their future. "They would like to show, acting for this cause, that education is serious and it requires sacrifice and altruism, submission, and resignation."[86]

There is no doubt that the architect of this devotion to humanity and a sound understanding of trusting in God (*tawakkul*) is Fethullah Gülen. But what has drawn a man who comes from the *madrasa* system into the field of modern education? Why would someone who is aging and has had a difficult medical history engage in such a marathon? Some people ask similar questions from a reverse angle: What does a religious person have to do with education? If he is a preacher or *hodja* (religious teacher), why does not he keep himself confined to his own specialization? These have been the questions asked by media groups and by various people from different sectors of society. These questions were answered in interviews held on various occasions, according to the context in which the questions were raised.

Gülen is almost the only person who has, both directly and indirectly, paid so much attention to the issue of education. In his sermons, conversations, articles, and essays, he has struggled to present the need to engage the masses in educational projects. He has tried to relay his message to all sectors of society, but especially to tradesmen and artisans who have come to listen to his sermons and lectures; he has exhorted them strongly to deal with the lack of proper education in the society.

In the near history of the Republic, the issue of education has been normally restricted to a handful of ideologues and politicians. Education has been a field over which only an enlightened group of people pondered, talked, debated and put forward projects. The large masses of society have not been permitted to participate in these discussions in any way. The matter of education has been regarded too important to entrust to the general public! That has been the general attitude of Turkish intellectuals. They could never think that a large community of tradesmen would mobilize their economic capacity for education without expecting any profit. As a matter of fact, the grassroots had never assumed any role in such political, educational, or socio-cultural projects. Fethullah Gülen challenged this perspective, and the elite character of its proponents. He argued that such a perspective alienates people from education, politics, and the state.

Gülen regards and defines the matter of education as the biggest problem of not only our country but also of contemporary modern civilization. He believes that the education of humankind is the foundation of faith. At the root of the modern education crisis lies the fragmentation of the once-harmonious heart and mind connection in education and scientific thinking. Gülen contends that the new education system will not be able quell this crisis unless it redefines the natural and inherent relationship between humanity, the cosmos, and God. For the last couple of centuries, modern scientific thought and education has turned all humane, social, and ideological relationships into profane objects, stripping them of their sacredness and ascribing to them a positivist nature. This situation has led to corruption and a spiritual crisis that society currently witnesses. One of the innovations developed by Gülen is his holistic outlook in regard to the relationship between human being, the cosmos, and God—namely the harmonious unity of mind and heart.[87] The colleges inspired by his ideas have questioned and overcome this extremely positivistic problem that deadlocks contemporary thought and education systems. It goes without saying that these schools do not offer their students a religious education. However, they do treat mind and heart simultaneously as the center of information and thought, and offer a system that views humans as existing in a harmonious relationship with the universe, society, and God. These schools work to create model individuals who are confident in themselves and the future; who are at peace with their own personality; who are respectful of their traditions, the roots of their faith, and their social identity; and who are open to modern scientific thought, innovation, and change. That is why, everywhere they have been opened, these colleges represent a new voice in education, and an excellent model of successful, hard-working, and open-minded students.

In addition, these colleges have changed the clumsy understanding of education as it was defined by blind repetition, which was based on memorization of definite patterns. The Turkish education system is still mostly dependent on memorization. It is under the yoke of formal logic in many fields. The educational program at these schools established a mathematical and experimental form of logic, and a progressive method that is not based on memorization or repetition. They have brought a new dynamism to education. They have transformed the formerly stagnant and lazy attitude of Turkish education, improving and highlighting student learning in all subjects.

Another significant development emerging from these schools is in the realm of student-teacher, school-parent, and student-student relationships. The colleges promote an emotional, sincere, and heartfelt order of relations between all the people involved in a student's education. From this point of view, the colleges have reproduced genuine and positive relations between the family, street, and community, and they have adapted these relations to modern conditions. They reconstruct the former self-sacrificing "person of society," who is totally devoted to his or her nation and to humanity, and who is the hero of love and affection. In this era, when selfishness, egotism and materialism prevail, this is a remarkable achievement. In a time dominated by the primacy of material interests and idolization of personal, this new form of education is leading students to prefer the profession of teaching over all others. While there are highly respected occupations in aviation, computer and industrial engineering, medicine, etc., which provide social status and prestige, these people choose teaching.[88] These teachers take these merits with them wherever they go. Each of them thus becomes "an ambassador of culture." Many of the places they go are not even suitable for tourists; but despite material deprivation, these teachers meet their surroundings with high spirit. They establish warm relations with local people in those countries, and thus form a historic bridge. It is difficult to gauge the impact this bridge will have on behalf of Turkey, but it is not difficult to predict that the schools will enable Turkey and the co-operating countries the possibility of establishing and improving broad relations on a humane and social basis.

THE COLLEGES AND DIALOGUE BETWEEN CIVILIZATIONS

An outgrowth of these schools' success is the activities of inter-civilizational dialogue that emerge from a humble, self-sacrificing circle. These schools, with their teaching and administrative staff, strive to bring people of diverse religions, cultures, and civilizations to common understandings. It lays the cornerstone and foundation of dialogue. By raising people who are consistent with moral, humane, and social values, and who can welcome diversity, these schools establish a comprehensive infrastructure for future inter-civilizational dialogue. A human being who is harmonious with various cultural fibers is the most basic element of a culture of reconciliation. The idea that a person is open to various cultural tissues and diversity, of course, does not signify swaying, or being alienated, from one's origins. Both dialogue and reconciliation refer to a broad, common spectrum of social space that allows people to live together on the basis of mutual respect without denying each person's foundations for existence. Otherwise, it is not an activity of complete participation. In this respect, economic and social exploitation, as well as cultural assimilation, are definitely contrary to the aim of dialogue and reconciliation.

Despite our concerns, we are exposed to a comprehensive web of relations dictated by the processes of "globalization." Globalization, in every aspect, has brought and piled up pluralism and has brought "the other," the sum of our fears, to the doorstep of our traditional religious-national system. Directly and indirectly, this process affects us all and affects all of our social relations. We should redefine different cultural tissues through a viable platform, without hostility, crisis, or conflict. Not only in the political and ethnic sense, but also in the sense of cultural and social fiber, Anatolia constituted a mosaic of civilizations. While the concept of a mosaic naturally brings to mind a sense of political and ideological anxieties, Anatolia is really one of the rare geographical areas which sustained a culture of dialogue in its history. As to dialogue and tolerance, men of wisdom, such as Yesevi, Rumi, and Yunus, who all embodied dialogue and tolerance in their life experiences, serve as sources from which these colleges may derive inspiration and guidance. Externally, the colleges feed themselves from these sources. They bear this spirit everywhere they go with their large number of teachers. This is why some people describe this movement as the manifestation of contemporary Turkish humanism.

In the West, many have located this movement within the framework of Turkish Sufism. While neither "Sufism" nor "humanism" define the colleges fully, it is true that self-sacrifice, sincerity, and transcendental human values ring with Sufi and humanist tunes.[89] However, the education system of the colleges is directed towards a larger segment of society and toward the foundation of knowledge. In contrast, both Sufi ideals and humanism refer to narrow and more stagnant roots. Generally speaking, Sufism displays an exclusionary attitude against worldly and technological progress. In this sense, it establishes a one-sided relation between matter and spirit. As to humanism, it has a weak and frail willpower against social processes; human beings exhibit a passive attitude, not an active being, against society and events. In the education system of these schools, a person is viewed as enterprising and active in social processes. The schools adhere to a model that pursues a balance between the material world and the spiritual, without reducing one to the other, in order to construct an active model that can bear the responsibility of societal and cultural dialogue.

Beyond any doubt, many things can be said in regard to the philosophical and ideological roots of the schools. We should bear in mind that we encounter a system that places action before ideas and intellectual design. I feel the need to emphasize this point because intellectual and mental speculations and definitions often run the risk of not overlapping with practice. In an ideological or mental framework, the social attitude of the movement may constitute a broad impact that far exceeds the borders of this framework. A philosophical framework drawn today may not work tomorrow, as social life practices may bring new developments. Because of this, it is more consistent to look at the educational activities of this movement in light of its social practice, rather than through the narrow perspective of finely designed, frozen philosophical and ideological concepts.

TEACHERS OF WISDOM, KNOWLEDGE OF GOD, AND DIALOGUE

In Gülen's thought, the teacher is crucially important because he or she prepares the individual and society for the future. Traditionally, teachers were the holy carriers of the Muslim community. They toiled under social and human burden of all types, and thus, their power and social respect were both part of their social identity. The corruption of the educational system affected teachers first. As they lost their quality and social influence, the quality of all people descended with them. Here, the manner of action that defines Gülen seeks to honor the teaching profession and to facilitate the reappearance of the teacher on the stage of history. Gülen's vision is bold and broad in its scope; his vision of the teacher is of someone defined by a healthy balance between material and spiritual yearnings, and of someone who has a sacrificing and sincere identity. For Gülen, such a teacher has never been so necessary in any period in history.

In a way, Gülen has awakened a sleeping giant. It can be said that it is impossible to analyze the Gülen movement unless you properly understand the immensity of the education campaign and the personnel behind it. The teacher has assumed a central role in his system. Teachers are both the transmitters of a virtuous society and examples of the devoted individual, of tolerance and dialogue. As mentioned before, Gülen inspired both a new educational system and a new example of devotion. This new and vast experience is founded in Gülen's blend of Sufi, humanistic, and universalistic fibers. The dedication of these teachers is rooted in their love for humanity and their adaptability to other cultures and geographies. Let's follow Gülen's views on the characteristics and significance of the teachers who have spread humanistic virtue, dedication, and bravery across the world:

> From birth until death, the teacher is a holy master who gives shape to the world throughout one's life. On earth, there is no equal to him in guiding his nation to their fate, in refining their ethics and their characteristics, and in infusing his nation with the awareness of eternity.
>
> The influence of the teacher on the individual far exceeds the one exerted by his parents and by society. In fact, it is the teacher who kneads the mother, the father, and all members of society. If he is not involved in the kneading of any piece of dough, it is left formless.
>
> The teacher is a hand, a tongue, God uses to exalt or humiliate humanity. Yes, a nomadic community that found its instructor was sublimed as high as angels and they all ascended to the rank of being teachers for humanity.[90] With a good teacher, Macedonia raised a great conqueror; Anatolia reached its prosperous era; and people like Fatih Sultan Mehmet opened a new age thanks to their teachers. Yavuz (Selim I), a man of great discipline and order, as well as hundreds more like him, was the fortunate apprentice of an eminent teacher.
>
> In a teacher's hands, metals are purified and then turned into solid gold and bright silver. In this mystic hand, the crudest and the most worthless things become invaluable diamonds. No factory can work as fast and as systematic as the teacher does. No one but the teacher can convey the depth of the emotional spectrum to those around him and become a part of their existence.
>
> The teacher is the interpreter of all substances that ooze from the unsurpassable climaxes of the world of secrets; he is the voice and the word for undetectable motions in the world

of existence. Through him, people rise like clouds and descend as blessings.

The most trustworthy of the worlds beyond the heavens was a master (Gabriel), and the soul who opened his chest to the master's message was the greatest of teachers (the Prophet). He was the instructor of both the individual and the community, and we all became indebted to him and to the profession of teaching... Today, whatever we know and whatever is known all comes from him; the rest is just rumor...

The teachers manifested themselves sometimes as philosophers, sometimes as ascetics, and at times, as dervishes, and they stamped their presence in their times. Each of them, however, took different forms in proportion to the extent they benefited from the "truth." In early periods, the lovers of wisdom repeated the melodies that belonged to the Prophets. The scholastic scientists and teachers of the Middle Ages added "positivism" to their hymns. In the same age, teachers of the East were in pursuit of discovering the nature of human being and awakening him to his own reality with the divine decree they had in their hands.

After the Renaissance, along with everything, the teacher also changed. He became a callow lover who blindly lost himself in the events. His only pursuit was his own interest, passionately devoted to nothing else but a new discovery or invention as he rushed between his workbench at home and the workshop at the market. During this period, leaders never became teachers for their society. In this era, the masses followed certain directions, as they were deceived with excessive inculcation and exhibitions—they never saw teachers as their leaders. As a matter of fact, at the wedding night of this rebirth, the heart was enslaved by Mephistopheles.

Later came the banal teachers of materialism, who tried to explain everything as functions of matter to be used for technical means. From the telescope to the microscope, these technologies became the means by which humanity defined nebula and penetrated x-rays into particles. At that age, nothing was done in the name of sublimation, and thus it is hard to refer to such teachers in a positive way. However, this highly hard and dark period did not last long, and now has begun a new time of curiosity and exploration.

After a handful of bandits committed serious crimes against humankind, today's army of knowledge and gnosis are suspicious about the recent past. They long to find out the causes and effects of knowledge and to return the teaching profession to the high status it deserves. These teachers will excite the hearts and sharpen the will of society, and they will enlighten minds and strengthen hearts. Under the guidance of such teachers, it will be possible for students to get in touch with the beyond. Thanks to those messages that come from the sublime, students will receive inspirations that are many times beyond their understanding. In fact, science that does not help the student get in touch with the "Absolute" will not shed light upon matter or bring sublime synthesis. Such science leads the heart to suspicion, and drowns the heart with uncertainty. If the teacher puts the student into this situation, he cannot be named a teacher anymore; he is either a non-believer or a skeptic.

For that reason, for a long time, the purest and the most truthful lesson has been represented by the community of prophets, who have never deceived nor been deceived. The school of prophets is open to everyone of all ages, and it covers all spheres of life. The classroom of this school can be anywhere, and everyone has the potential to be either the teacher or the lucky student who drinks from this spring of knowledge.

The state is an academy where the chieftains give and attend lectures. At this great school, which is open to every one, the great statesmen have the spirit and the awareness of statesmanship. This state has no resemblance to Plato's state ruled by philosophers, or to Bodin's state, an opposite form of Plato's. This is a generic state. And this state's foremost feature is that the statesmen have come to that level, at every step in their upward development, from the statesmen's apprenticeship to the stage where they are senior authorities, learning abundantly from life and events. If they did not pass through some levels, and without getting united with the universe, there would be ridiculous results, like the desire to command from the rank of private, or to fill the place of commander-in-chief. Such a situation is the greatest calamity for a nation.

With his sublime feelings, Brahman was an immortal teacher to his followers' hearts. Buddha, on the difficult path to Nirvana, was another exemplary teacher with clean feelings. Confucius was a teacher of ethics; Hormizd was a teacher pointing the secrets of eternity. And Omars, who were crystallized with the sublime Existence, became teachers thanks to their master. Time could not erode these, and social turmoil would not allow us forget these great teachers, who all still live in people's hearts. Who knows, perhaps one day, humanity will ultimately arrive at this eternal understanding.

The endeavor of our people is to reorganize themselves by finding their real teachers and masters. This would surely bring surprising results. It is hoped that today's teachers would have the spirit of conquerors and discoverers. By observing holy principles and thoughts, a teacher should fulfill his duty fit for the perfect synthesizers: may he consider Nizam al-Mulk and Alp Arslan together, and Fatih and Akshamsaddin side by side; may he not separate Zenbilli from Yavuz; may he not forget Pascal in Ghazali's illuminated skies. While whirling in Rumi's magical words, he is not to neglect to pay a visit to the lab, so as to send his greetings to Pasteur. In short, he should accept the wholeness of body and soul as an emblem.

Countless greetings to those teachers who suffer in order to train and elevate their generations![91]

Gülen emphasizes the positive contribution of the teachers to the history of human civilization. It seems that his concept of a teacher goes far beyond our conceptions of a teacher. For him, the teacher is history. He appears to sum up all of human history from the perspective of a teacher. In his mind, the teacher symbolizes an army of knowledge that ranges from nomadism to civil society, from philosophy to asceticism, and from the dervishes to statesmen. Gülen also explains the historic role of the teacher from ancient Greek philosophy to old Indian Buddhism, from the Judeo-Christian tradition to the European Renaissance, and from our civilization to modern positivist understandings to rewrite the history through the perspective of the teacher. According to Gülen, only an inquisitive and synthesizing army of knowledge can change the course of a corrupted human civilization that is plagued by an unbalanced equilibrium in society. The teacher is central to this vision. Taking a look at the role attributed to the teacher, our mind spontaneously makes an association to the sacred. His imagination stirs so fast and freely that the curves of human history are viewed as sanctification of this concept. According to him, the teacher is literally a holy person. Since teachers share a significant portion of the role of prophets, is the teacher who receives a holy rank. Generally speaking, a new society and a new civilization can only be achieved via the efforts of a serious army of educators based soundly within the teaching profession. For that reason, Gülen frequently speaks of the necessity of such a staff of erudition.

Of course, there are two elements needed to materialize this ideal: the school and the teacher. Gülen considers the school to be a place that combines the different experiences of humanity in unity, and thus, it is a place that protects him from various mental and practical disorders. This, indeed, reflects the picture of the school in his mind. He envisages a veritable laboratory. To his eye, it is not merely a place where teachers and students pay a visit and leave for a considerable part of their lives. The school is a place to subject the teacher and the student to a chemical transformation; it is a laboratory that prepares them to solve all the problems of humanity and civilization. The school is an institution that forms both the child and the teacher, and that shapes the social and ecological environment:

> In the beginning of every academic year we cannot help but think about the school and the teacher. How can we not? The school is an essential laboratory, our courses are the elixir of life, and the teacher is the heroic savant of this mystical infirmary.
>
> School is a place for learning, where we learn about this world as well as the next. As a matter of fact, life itself is a school. But we learn about life at school.
>
> The school enlightens the crucial events of society by casting rays of knowledge upon them, by enabling students to perceive their environments. At the same time, it helps us understand the secret of existence and events. It shows humanity the holistic thought and the integrity of contemplation. It helps us see unity in plurality. In this sense, the school is more like a temple, and that temple's saints are the teachers.
>
> A good school that makes the individual develop his feelings of virtue in an angelic pavilion that endows its attendants with

spiritual sublimity. Not every school is the same, however; some buildings look wrecked, and thus its students become rough. Some may even become monsters, the products of centipede dens. People have been contorted before these homes of snakes and scorpions for many centuries.

A real teacher protects the pure and healthy seed. His duty is to look after the good and sound, to show ideals, and to direct him in the face of new developments and calamities.

Like a river flowing from all directions, life gains its purpose at school. Similarly, the child finds out the secrets about his own self at school. Like an untidy river flowing around but gathering in a narrow passage and looking with grandeur, or the pure vital liquid crystallizing and establishing an affinity with sun rays, the child attains unity in plurality in the same way that fruit manifests the unity of all the parts of a tree.

It is supposed to be that the school occupies only a small part of human being's life; in fact, it is a home with the duty of showing all the disharmonious things in the school of the universe. It is a home that offers the possibility of studying all the time; it is a home that speaks even when it is silent. For that reason, while it seems to occupy a small portion of life, it is a symbolic home that dominates all times and makes all happenings listen to it. Any student attending school as an apprentice will recite his lesson throughout his life. The things adopted there may have been products of one's imagination, a dream, a reality, or a skill. The essential matter is that whatever is achieved is part of a mystic key that can open locked doors and can lead the way to virtue.

At school, science is absorbed into the self; by means of this, the student passes over the borders of the solid material world and, in a way, is elevated to the borders of eternity. Science not having been integrated into the self is a burden on the back of the human being, an embarrassing one. Such knowledge carries with it certain responsibility; science can appear like Satan, who keeps confusing the consciousness. Any incomplete learning that does not promise one's ascension to the soul and to enlightenment is a rasping file and a blow dealt to the heart.

The best education a school can give consists of bringing external events and internal knowledge side-by-side. In this school, the teacher is an external guide, but he is experience in our soul. It is for certain that the greatest unchangeable science and the most truthful recitation of a lesson is life itself. For those who do not know how to learn from it, however, teachers are needed to serve as intermediaries who bridge life and the self, and who interpret what is dark from what is light.

Newspapers, books, television, and radio are all likely to teach something to people. But they are never able to teach real life and its experience for human being. By gaining the hearts of the students with different means, against all pain and torment every day, and by leaving inerasable tracks in their minds with his lessons as well as with his behavior, the teacher resides in a place that cannot be replaced by any other person. It is for that reason that even if the student learns something from the facilitating methods of the West, no examples of virtue will be presented and purpose in science be taught. These can be taught only by a teacher whose face shines with the truth, whose gazes are extremely profound, and who refines everything he will give in his heart.

If the apostles had not seen the Messiah Christ teaching despite the threat of being crucified, how would they smile as they were being thrown to the lions? If they did not see the greatest guide of all time praying others to be soft-hearted even when he was wounded and bleeding, how would they have known that there is coolness and peace even in flames?

A good lesson is one that is learned at school before a teacher. Such a course not only gives him something but also promotes him to the presence of the unknown and bestows upon him infinity. To the student in this class, every incident is embroidered upon the invisible world; He is the observer of truth behind the mobile slabs.

In such a school, no one can match the utility of the teacher. How could they? Teachers raise their students to the stars and give them breath; they take them beyond the borders they live within.

The real teacher is a person who can see through the veils over the natural phenomena, who establishes a relation between life and conscience, like a conductor discharging to a receiver, hearing the truth out of anything, trying to interpret it in any language, and explaining it to the others.

Rousseau's master was conscience. For Kant, it was a combination of conscience and reason. In the school of Rumi and Yunus, the master is the Prophet Muhammad, peace be upon him . . . The Qur'an is an anthology of sayings and hymns from this divine lesson, a collection of mysterious sayings that silence all other words and that show the Unity within multiplicity.[92]

. . ,

If only we could have taught our people how to express constructive, enlightening criticism. If only we could have taken lessons from the past and from the recurring events in history . . .

Unless the teacher is beneficial; if the school does not give crucial lessons; an if the books do not reflect the mystery crystallized in the heart of the universe, then that teacher is pitiful, that school is in darkness, and those who attend that school are ill-fated. And if the teacher is on his way to get to know the material and the phenomena with the lens in his hand; if the book emits radiance and functions like an electron-microscope; and if the school works as a laboratory on this mysterious fair, then the teacher is happy, the school is an enlightened place, and the students are very fortunate.

Now I wonder, has the teacher been able to perform his duty in our recent past? Could he assure the enlightenment of his students' souls and their association with the universe? Could he put radiance into their hearts and equip them with lofty ideals? Could he teach them life in every aspect and save their souls from humiliation? Could he make them love books and school, and introduce them to the great aim of science?[93]

To us, the real teacher and guide is the fortunate person who, with the faculty and aptitude to become anything, teaches the truth to all men born into this world, who makes others think positively, who excites their hearts and gives wings to their souls, who unblocks all the impeding darkness, and who takes them to the illuminated vents.

How blessed the teacher is who devotes himself to his students, who follows them step-by-step, in every turn of their life, and who feels exalted by elevating them to humanity; only such a teacher is able to show them the absolute truth with the lens of science, sometimes charged like thunderbolts— one who illuminates his students hearts, and who beams with light as he softens their souls![94]

One cannot be called a teacher if, in the name of science, he leaves his students in doubt; nor can a school be called a school if a student, with the solemnity of a lab, is directed to false outcomes.[95]

This sublime task must be meticulously adopted in every national institution, from the school to the temple, and as far as it is possible, to all voluntary and intellectual souls who have attained unity of the mind and the heart. It is their mission to accomplish these goals because the teacher and the guide is a mature person who has, in the first place, achieved the truth within his soul. Only then is he capable of discharging that truth from his bosom to the hearts of his apprentices. Souls who have not illuminated themselves with the Divine rays that arrive from all corners of the universe have little means by which to elevate the masses to the level of humanity; likewise, confused minds who have surrendered to their doubts have little means by which to give an education to their students. At most, the people in institutions where power is represented find consolation in old epics and folk songs; they take refuge behind folklore and ceremonies in the name of religion, and they howl with others' legends in regard to the human being's relationship with the Creator. They are enraptured by them; but they can never become the ones who can trigger inspirations, who raise souls, and who encourage hearts.[96]

We are charged with the responsibility of endowing our world with a fresh, new spirit, woven from a love of faith, a love for our fellow human beings, and a love of freedom. We have further been charged with the responsibility for being ourselves, connected to the principle of these three loves, and for preparing the ground for the shoots, the pure roots of the blessed tree of Paradise, so that it will be nurtured and grow in the loam of these loves. This, of course, depends on the existence of heroes who will take responsibility for, and protect, the country's destiny and the history, religion, traditions, culture, and all sacred things that belong to the people; this will depend on heroes who are absolutely full of a love for science and knowledge, burgeoning with the thought of improvement and construction, sincere and devout beyond measure, patriotic and responsible, and, therefore, always conscientiously at work, in charge, and on duty. Thanks to these heroes and their sincere efforts, our system of thoughts and understanding, and the fruit of these, will prevail with our people; the sense of devoting oneself to others and to the community will gain prominence; the understanding of the division of labor, the management of time, and assisting and liaising with one another will be revived; all relationships of authority-subject, employer-employee, landlord-tenant, landowner-peasant, artist-admirer, attorney-client, and teacher-student will become different aspects of the unity of the whole; and all this will come about once more, as all our expectations from ages past will come true, one-by-one. We now live in an era in which our dreams are being realized, and we believe that with good timing, each of the responsibilities of the age will have been accomplished by the time its day arrives.[97]

. . . From this point of view, our most crucial aim is to light the fire of "making others live" in the hearts of our fellow countrymen, so as to dispose the alien thoughts that intervene between them and their ideals. We must then activate their inert energy, and with motivation and disciplined activity, make them walk towards their historical ideal. In such a mobilization, it is an utmost necessity to meet people from all walks of life—the intellectual, the artisan, the peasant, the city-dweller, the student, the teacher, the preacher, etc.—on common denominators that can serve as an orbit for this collective movement. Among such common denominators, we can list the following: elevating our country to a position where it can act in a balancing role among other world states; and nourishing our society with the understanding that love for truth and the desire for learning and research can be the means to rise to the Divine . . .[98]

CHAPTER FOUR

Religious Perspective

RELIGIOUS PERSPECTIVE

ISLAMIC ORIGINS OF COMMUNITY

I titled this section as such because Western analyses of community are dependent, in many respects upon Western social and historical values. Sociological analyses that are so contingent upon external influences and cultural changes may not somehow encompass the survival of communities in Muslim societies. Even the most astute Western analysts cannot explain about Muslim communities without employing Western concepts.

In both Tönnies and Weber, community indicates social disintegration and/or disengagement. The Muslim world, however, has not experienced such a social disintegration or disengagement in its traditional social structure. Furthermore the factors that form community ties in Muslim societies never resemble tribal or clannish ties. Excessive stress over tribal, clannish, and racial ties is considered in Islam as part of the "tradition of ignorance" (*jahiliyya*). The prophetic saying expresses that Islam completely excludes all kinds of fanaticism.[1] The obvious reason for this is that such ties obstruct the development of relational networks between Muslims and the broader society. All kinds of ignorance are rejected because they cause excessive stress over sub-identities, blood feuds, and enmity.[2]

Despite the decisive attitude of Islam against these fanatical ties, they have seriously busied Muslim societies after the demise of the Prophet Muhammad, peace be upon him. Nevertheless, tribal and clannish movements never managed to destroy or discriminate in Muslim societies. At least these identities have never been religiously justified; for the same reason it is not possible to analyze the communion of Muslim societies as a relational form of feudal order or as a form of agricultural society.

The foundations that form the spirit of unity and solidarity in Muslim communities can only be explained by Islamic social and religious practices. Islam encourages charity, common good, establishing human, moral, and social benefit. It advocates production and development while urging competition between groups and communities in organized forms.[3]

Generally speaking, as individuals, humans are reluctant to partake in charity works. Even if they are willing to do charity, they are more inclined to realize this in an organizational and systematical way. Since individuals are occupied with their personal interests and livelihoods, charity works on behalf of society are most of the time ignored. Motivations for charity do not usually come to the surface unless there is necessity or an emergency.[4]

On the other hand each society may indoctrinate common ideals about the future of their society. This activity is executed extensively and systematically, and in each generation, it becomes a new tradition. The tradition refers to individuals' subconscious. However, this subconscious may not produce common consciousness in each period and for each individual at the same level. Social disintegration takes place as long as this conscious deteriorates. Islam, as religion and civilization, addresses the social acts of Muslim societies as well as constructing their subconscious. It constantly renovates the images of goodness in society and in individuals by encouraging goodness, self-sacrifice, and solidarity. Behind civil foundations lies this awareness of goodness in Muslim societies.

Here is the legitimacy and *raison d'être* of Muslim communities. The phenomenon of Muslim community is an organization of the universal good in the society. Community addresses the good feelings of Muslim individuals; and it brings them to a spirit of contest in charity, goodness, and well-being. Humans tend to be more desirous towards collective encouragement and goodness, solidarity and cooperation.

When done individually, the charity giver often does not see where his goodness materializes within the endless layers of society. Even he cannot estimate the form his goodness might take through needs and relations. In communal activities, however, each contribution immediately materializes. In communal life, goodness, common sense, ideal, sacrifice, and empathy are concrete. For this, it is more convincing and effective. In communities individuals observe more quickly how their sacrifice becomes concrete. Mass psychology and acting as a group have a strong magnetic power over individuals. Although naturally good feelings prevail in human beings, he inclines more to selfish feelings. If there is not a serious encouragement to direct his desire to sacrifice, his inclination to give would be very weak. Community socializes all the selfish feelings. It saves individuals from the maelstrom of selfishness, stinginess, and hedonism. It raises each sense, aptitude, feeling, and idea to the level of virtue and merit. This is the essence of the community in Muslim society.

Defined as such, the ideal Muslim community has a collective personality (*şahs-ı manevi*). In a way, it is a spiritual corporation. It tries to direct even the most corporeal senses to spirituality and eternity. God's consent and pleasure is the principal motive and reason of all sacrifices and altruism. Any concept of worldly reward is deemed to be a low and even undesirable consideration. Be it individual or social, all acts within the community have to be intertwined with God's consent. Any worldly interest, individual or family, would undermine this ideal.

I will touch upon a point here. The social identity of community depends upon spread of goodness and charity. Participation to the community for these works is solely civil and voluntary. We should separate this from the institution of *"hisba"* which we have seen in Muslim societies throughout Islamic history. *Hisba* was a bureaucratically established formal institution seeking to serve as an arm of the local municipality. Communities are volunteer establishments that emerge within the society. Force, be it in the form of psychological or material suppression and/or compulsion, is not tolerated within the sphere of community.

In Islamic history, historical and social situations produced volunteer and civil communities. Sub-institutions like charity associations, foundations (*waqf*), guilds etc. undertake social functions similar to those of communities, and works are fulfilled in the spirit of social worship.

Muslim communities are Islamic social realities that have, in any case, appeared in new formats in modern times. Most of them have reproduced a different social form of religious organization. The emergence of today's communities has more to do with the political disintegration of the Islamic world. In Muslim societies, unlike the West, cooperative spirit is predominant rather than rational spirit. In Islamic history, therefore, Muslim communities were the outcome of subjective political and social conditions and they subsequently cannot be analyzed with Western communal concepts.

The major fault of Orientalists like Montgomery Watt etc., including sociologists, is that they evaluate schools of thought, and communities in Islamic history as oppositions to the Muslim tradition from the outside, opposition that sought to confront general Muslim orthodoxy. Yet the fact is on the contrary; in Islamic history emerging movements, with few marginal exceptions, never thought to exist at the expense of the Qur'an and the *Sunna*, the main sources of Islamic knowledge. Even the most marginal movements that exclude much of Islam's social tradition feel themselves to be supported by these two sources in some fashion. Movements in Muslim societies sought (and seek) to expand from within, not search for external identities.

Western analyses continually try to observe a clash between classes in Muslim societies, be that clash in the form of tribe, clan, schools of thought, or between communities. For them these elements are the carriers of clash and social dispute. They think that while in the West class conflict stands for a search of political or social identity, in Muslim societies this search realizes itself on the base of groups and communities. This analogy is rather simple and faulty since it has no Muslim social or historical foundation from which to build upon. As stated earlier, even the most extreme movement express itself within the framework of a general Islamic identity. Without accepting and understanding the central place of the Qur'an in Muslim societies, it would not be possible to explain the individual and societal nature of Muslims.

Gülen's perception of community

Gülen perceives the existence of community on the base from which one builds an effort of "service to God and people." Human existence in the world has two main objectives: First, "servant-hood" to God; second, "exalting the word of God" (*i'la-yı kelime-tullah*); that is to say, learning about God and teaching others in this respect. These two are the most essential elements that define a Muslim's mission in this world. All his personal, social, and ethical acts are connected to these two fundamental principles. Exalting the word of God as a noble ideal goes beyond the capacity of individual effort; single acts of good-will and sacrifices in this direction are not enough. Conveying this message to the masses requires the existence of an orderly community. The Holy Qur'an describes all believers as being part of a super identity that forms around the consciousness of the "*umma*." Though the term "*umma*" expresses Muslim societies in general, it is an abstract concept. Communities, in one sense, partly undertake social functions of the *umma* because they create a group that exceeds personal wills. From this point of view, the *umma* has always been a point of emphasis in Muslim societies. Thus says Gülen, "The idea of community is crucial. An idea of community in the sense of rational, logical, and spiritual unity where each individual assigns his personal thoughts and feelings to a noble ideal."[5]

Community is a rational, logical, spiritual, and psychological unity. It is a voluntary choice. Community is also a moral group. It never pressures anybody. It is solely bound to the voluntary and rational choice of individuals: "[i]n fact the real moral society is the one that promises worldly and otherworldly happiness and surrender to a noble ideal with their free will. In a society such this, the unifying faith, the softening love and the eminence of aim would not allow negativities out of egoism so that immorality would grow up in this body . . ."[6]

Community is the crucible in which individuals melt their ego, personal interests, motives, and worries one by one, and join a collective body. By melting into the crucible of community, all of one's individualistic and hedonistic attitudes become socialized. Egoism is immoral. Each human being has personal aspects peculiar to his or her individual nature; however his or her existence develops as a member of a social setting. His personality and morality form in society: "We cannot talk of morality or immorality for those who live in solitude from the society. For Islam, enduring with misfortunes that originate from living in society is equal to jihad."[7]

In the quote above, Gülen refers to the hadith according to which a person who mixes with people and endures misfortunes that arise from being with them is superior to the one who does not.[8] There is a subtle point here; mixing in the society is sometimes painful. In society thousands of different types of people live together. Some have moral, physical, and/or personality problems. There are some individuals who do not care about anything save fulfilling their own interests and pleasures. For such people, personal choices take precedence over the choices of others. Another's desire is only important to the point that it strengthens and raises one's own desires. Some treat others contemptuously and denigrate them. Some prefer to rule and oppress others. In a society there are endless differences in flavor and style. This creates many problems. When these differences are associated with personal interests, social life becomes unbearable. Despite all of these, the Prophet, peace be upon him, proclaims that *the best of humankind is the one who is with others*; this is considered "jihad." The basic function of community is to prepare individuals for society and to socialize them and their personal ability, aptitude, and choices. "A life fashioned with faith, love, and sincerity results in such transcendence that this softens and dissolves each individual and his or her personal characteristics in the society; while keeping on as he is, he becomes universal and attains the richness of being an ocean when he was a drop, and of being a sun when he was an atom."[9] Here the important aspect of community comes on the scene; individuals do not give up their personal abilities and characteristics. On the contrary, they stay as themselves and they get rich with the peculiarities developed via the spiritual entity of the community.

Many modern theories allude to the development of a conflict between individual and social identity. This myth of "conflict" is positioned behind the personality and identity problems created by modernity. Eventually, either individual identity or formal social identity is overemphasized. Thus new identity and inequality problems emerge from this gap formed by personal identity and social integrity.

Modern Muslim communities, on the contrary, do not aim to dissolve the personal identities of its members. Quite the opposite, it broadens and enriches them. In a sense, modern Muslim communities socialize personal identities by forming them around a sublime and noble ideal. Sincerity, affection, worship, and obedience mature humans as individuals, and escort them to the doors of a kind of transcendence. Unable to merge with societal ideals a person cannot become a perfect human being (*insan al-kamil*). Perfect humanity is only realized in society through noble values and ideals.

Gülen constantly stresses the significance of community by its role in facilitating the training of individuals in society with spiritual discipline and consciousness of God:

Serving on this path is the noblest of all services; the mission is only God's content; and the consequence is happiness in the other world. Even if a minor interest of either the person or the community is interfused into this genuine consideration, all eternal links that bequeath life to individuals and to the community will detach. This detachment results in the divergence of the individual from the main track, the community moves into shock and a vicious circle of failure starts; in fact this path presents a high possibility of victory.

As personal desires, ambitions, and worries should not be present in a community, (because all links and works are entirely connected to God the Almighty) so too should the individual cease his focus on short term ideals and dreams. A real community is a group of people who devote themselves to eternity so that, from Bediüzzaman's perspective, they work for God, start for God, speak for God, and meet for God; act for God, and thus their seconds become as long as years and they stamped this temporary worldly presence with the seal of eternity. Yes, all their works are exceptionally hearty, ingenious, and directed toward eternity.

In this manner one can say that not every crowd can be considered a community. When members are opposed to each other, their multitude will dwindle like the multiplication of fractional numbers. However, the companions of the prophets who were endowed with community spirit had been able to realize what was expected from a powerful community despite being small in quantity. All the same, it would not be an exaggeration at all to accept Abu Bakr (the first Caliph) and Umar (the second Caliph) as a community and nation by themselves. The apostles of Jesus can be perceived more powerful than huge armies. In fact throughout history, these types of mature minorities have been more powerful and more productive than great masses.

On the other hand, love of morality is the most important mechanism by which one can discipline spiritual life, and it is the most significant element of social stability and harmony. Virtues like righteousness, truthfulness, conscientiousness, and respecting others are the essence of morality and are fundamental dynamics of spirit.

If we exclude the last centuries, the moral insight we have inherited from our national history—is so rich and sound that it might lead us to the front of all nations. If we could discipline our near future according to this insight, many national problems would be naturally overcome and we would be able to think soundly, work more efficiently, walk speedier and more harmoniously; we would be more practical and obviously we would fill the century long gap in our life more swiftly.[10]

THE SPIRITUAL LIFE IN ISLAM

a. Sufism, spiritual orders, and community

There is no record for the existence of spiritual orders, (*tariqa*), as a social phenomenon, in Muslim history during the time of the Companions and their followers (*tabiun*). The last half of the period of *tabiun* and the subsequent century is when the first Sufis appeared. Yet during these two centuries, Sufism was more in the form of personal ascetic experiences, rather than a social phenomenon. A Sufi, like a philosopher, is one who seeks "*the truth.*" The Sufi's search for truth takes place in the domains of willpower, conscience, and heart; in other words the realm of absolute freedom.

The non-Sufi philosopher rotates in a circle; he busies himself with disputes and struggles, disapprovals and predictions. In the end, what he attains is nothing but a truth without spirit with which he is unlikely to become one. The Sufi, however, enjoys a bounteous spiritual life. He reaches this happiness not through the knowledge of the truth, but by his desire to attain and unite with the truth. The Sufi speaks with a particular language using symbols and allusions in a manner which can be understood only by those who had the same experience. In this realm of spiritual and moral experiences philosophy has nothing to offer humankind.[11] The vision of pure philosophic reason about the esoteric nature of a Sufi is limited. Islamic Sufi concepts like *hal* (state), *maqam* (station), *zawq* (pleasure), *kashf* (discovery) and *ilham* (inspiration) etc. are not products of the human intellect; they are products of a spiritual journey in the heart and the soul united with the knowledge of God (*marifa*). Sufism relies on insight and wisdom, not on knowledge. And this is attained only after one transcends his human, corporeal, and sensual qualities.

Sentimental faculties and conscience develop more than rational ones in Sufism. Sentimental profundity and intensity play an important role in a Sufi's life. The Sufi experience desires proximity between the lover and the beloved. Yet this proximity is not physical or bodily; it is experienced as joyous and spiritual state of proximity and union. The image of proximity designates reflection of the names and attributes of God. This is a kind of transcendental feeling. The existence of deep spiritual activity reveals a special experience which we call Sufi perception. The point where this perception starts is where our sense organs are exhausted. The conscious expansion of ego moves with intensity as it warily escalates to the upper strata of the perceptible. In a different dimension, the conscious heads toward a new transcendental spiritual object to which human nature will partake and re-unite by changing his personality. When this begins then commences a development in spiritual life. This is where Sufis find real life and existence.

Considered as a social phenomenon today the *tariqa*s first came into existence as Sufism. Although Sufism was open to external influences during the period of institutionalization, it existed in Islam's subjective, political, social, cultural, intellectual, and religious conditions before its institutionalization. The primary *raison d'être* of Sufism is a desire to live Islam more profoundly. In other words, Sufism is an effort to internalize a religious experience in one's soul and perceptions.

The first Muslim Sufis concentrated upon asceticism, and in doing so, they focused on verses that determine their relations with this world and the next, with their carnal self, and with God. This became more evident with new expansion generated by new conquests. Until new expansions, the internal dynamics of Islam focused on *fiqh* (jurisprudence), *kalam* (Islamic philosophy and theology), and *hadith* narration and compilation. Sufis extended this focus by trying to comprehend Qur'anic concepts such as *taqwa* (piety) and *muttaqi* (pious) more profoundly. The earliest authorities on *fiqh, kalam* and *hadith* were indeed pious people; however, Sufis viewed such scholars as busing themselves more with outward and formal aspects of Islam. For Sufis the *fiqh* method was dry and formalist, while *kalam* scholars merely engaged in philosophy using their rational mind, a practice that leaned on dry wit which has no experience regarding Divine Attributes, Names, and the Essence. Formalists on one hand and confused intellectuals on the other. This vacuum explains the *raison d'être* of Sufism and it sets the stage Sufism emerges.

On the basis of Sufism lies a struggle with the self, a purification of the heart, and a feeding of the soul. This is accomplished with prayers and remembrance, and with increasingly extra forms of worships. If the methodology of *fiqh* constitutes a fundamental part of Islamic civilization, social mind, worship, and transactions; Sufism should be viewed as the most important manifestation of Islamic spirituality. Sufism is not solely a lifestyle. It is at the same time a special perspective that determines how the Sufi should establish relations with his Lord, with himself, and with the whole universe and all its contents. But this perspective is a perfect worldview in wider and philosophical meaning. Sufis are distinct from the majority of Muslims for their view of world, and from *fiqh* and *kalam* scholars in regard to their view of religion, and from philosophers in regard to their ideas of God, humanity, and the universe.[12]

From the first period—the period of asceticism—onwards, Sufism formulated an interpretation of the worldly life in a way that is different from other perspectives. It departed from the religious understanding of *fuqaha* and *kalam* scholars as of the beginning of the third century (AH), and from philosophers after the third century.[13] In short, Sufism took on a revolutionary character. It has always had a profound effect on Muslims throughout the centuries.

Until the end of the second century, Sufi life and Sufi terminology was within the realm of individual practice than organized form. First Sufis dealt with concepts like heart (*qalb*), carnal self (*nafs*), conscience (*wijdan*), asceticism (*zuhd*), isolation (*uzlat*), piety (*taqwa*), fear (*khawf*), hope (*raja*), knowledge of God (*marifa*), perfect goodness (*ihsan*), affection (*mahabba*) and love (*ashq*), this worldly life (*dunya*) and hereafter (*akhira*). The next generation invented concepts like unity (*wahda*) and plurality (*kasra*), discovery (*kashf*) and witnessing (*shuhud*), annihilation (*fana*) and eternality (*baqa*), and deepened their spiritual experience around these concepts. In the third century AH, Sufism was first experienced in the form of isolation and travel, and then organized towards *hângah* (guesthouse), *ribât*, and *zaviyah*s (dervish lodges). In this period we observe rapid communization. Circles commenced in *masjids* turned to regular life under the direction of expert Sufi sheikhs in *hangah*s and *zawiya*s. Here Sufi schools formed under the leadership of the first founding sheikhs, and their followers learned the teachings and tenets of the community from these sheikhs in a special manner. These Sufi schools have become famous by the name of certain cities, thus revealing different central manifestations of Islamic spirituality. The first systematic Sufi terminology appeared in these centers.

Sufism progressed gradually towards a spiritual life and eventually formed formal rules as it progressed from an ascetic way of life with no fundamental principles and rules other than general principles established by the religion. Before transforming into a system with definite methods of asceticism, it experienced a transitory period. Here Sufism generally consisted of religious morality, and it focused of trying to understand the inner meaning and wisdom of worship. Though transitory, Sufis in this period observed a desire to establish a regular life in God's pleasure (*rida*), reliance (*tawakkul*), and asceticism (*zuhd*). Sufis like Ibrahim Edhem (d. 161 AH – 778 CE), Ma'ruf al-Karhi (d. 200 AH – 816 CE), Rabia al-Adawiyya (d. 185 AH – 801 CE), Fudayl b. Iyaz (d. 189 AH – 805 CE) were the leaders of this transitory period.

Following this period in the third and fourth centuries of Islam, Sufism entered its period of "ecstasy" (*vajd*), "discovery" (*kashf*), and "pleasure" (*zawk*). This was the golden age of Sufism. In the earlier transitory period, Sufism was considered a methodology that corresponded the science of *fiqh*, the former dealing mainly with inner meaning of worship, while the latter studied the outer forms of worship. In the new period, it became a self training practice and a new knowledge acquisition method that emerged alongside the learning methods of *kalam* scholars. Sufism was not only considered a method of training or combating the self, or as system of asceticism that focused on state and station (*hal* and *maqam*), this period also saw the emergence of considerations that shed light on new methods to acquire auxiliary elements of secret and perceptional knowledge.[14]

Thus started the progression of Sufism as a spiritual institution that was later called "*tariqa.*" Since the fourth century, following *tariqa* meant obeying entire teaching, manners, and ceremonies that were envisaged by one of these spiritual paths.

Sufism has two aspects. The first is related with practicing it with asceticism, worship, devotion to God, and leaving all bodily and worldly desires at bay by austerity (*riyada*) and sincere effort. The second aspect is spiritual. This pertains to the states the carnal self, the heart, and the soul go through. These states are generated by the practice of tough asceticism. In this aspect, everything is about ecstasy, pleasure, knowledge, affection, rapture etc. It is beyond the scope of this study to explore all aspects of Sufism. We do not touch on extremes and heterodoxies. Here is not the right place to discuss all of these. In sum, the organization of "*tariqa*" is a special aspect of Sufism. As expressed above, it is a form of subjective, material, social, political, intellectual, and religious conditions of Islam. Sufi approaches, of all kinds, have been significant aspects of Islamic spiritual life, and provided that they practice within the dictates of *sharia*, they are considered legitimate. Although there were some marginal and mystical teachings that went astray from the essentials and tradition of Islam, throughout Islamic history, Sufism survived as a way to transform spiritual unity in Muslim societies. It also provided potential for general Muslims to identify themselves with *sharia* laws and classical religious teachings.

Compared to *fiqh* and *kalam* methodology, it developed an easier way to integrate changing conditions of social life. According to Seyyed Hossein Nasr, "Sufism in Islam, has been over the centuries the hidden heart that has renewed the religion intellectually, spiritually, and ethically, and has played the greatest role in its spread and in its relation with other religions."[15]

b. Sufism in Gülen's thought

The Gülen movement is not a Sufi-oriented movement. Throughout his life, however, Gülen has often mentioned and emphasized Sufi concepts and terminology in his sermons, talks, and articles. In the strict sense of the word, he may personally be accepted as a "modern Sufi." His Sufism, however should be narrowed to the individual level. He does not rely on an ascetic understanding like forsaking the world or society as observed in some Sufi orders. To him, asceticism in the in the form of clergy is not something upon which Islam approves. This is because Islam is essentially a social religion. Gülen, however, disapproves of total social indulgence, that is, of people consuming all personal and material fancies. Asceticism neither forsakes the world nor does it teach one to engage in all his worldly desires. The Holy Qur'an teaches that we behave moderately in this manner. "Forsaking world" in the Qur'anic meaning is not escaping or quitting the world entirely. It is a discourse warning against total indulgence in this worldly life in ethics, in one's soul, and actual life.[16] The world has three aspects in the Muslim understanding: first, the aspect that faces itself; second, the aspect that faces His names (*asma*), i.e. as a place of manifestation of God's names and attributes; third, the aspect that faces the other world.[17] The first warning presented to humanity in the Qur'an is to be wary of the world's illusiveness and temporary nature.[18]

Of these three, the second and third constitute the center of the Sufi's perception of world. Sufism is not interested in the first aspect. The ascetic approach in the classical period of Sufism taught

Muslims to forsake the world in the name of Qur'anic roots and Muslim foundations. Disparaging this world is emphasized in many Qur'anic verses. From these verses, Sufis have systematized a disapproval of the world and have converted this to a practical and spiritual attitude. Indeed, as an outcome of this approach Sufis introduced a magnificent spiritual and cultural heritage equipped fully with experience and terminology. This cannot be overlooked. Yet in the first century of Islam—*sahaba* and *tabiun*—we observe many distinguished believers among the Companions who did not partake in this type of total abandonment/disengagement from the world. Total abandonment of the world was not relevant with the Companions, for they gave priority to spreading the message of God (*i'lay-i kalimatullah*) and teaching Islam (*tabligh* and *irshad*) over all their personal life, and over all aspects of their spiritual, moral, and social experience and welfare. For them, the most important aspect of life was not to systemize the revolution Islam generated in their souls, but to convey Islam to humanity, although they experienced the feeling in their heart at a personal level.

In the second and third Muslim centuries, conquests and encounters with foreign cultures resulted in a decisive inclination to worldliness and politicization problem. This transformation drove some to abandon the world and social life. In addition to this, during this time Islam gained status, form, and strength as an international civilization. The population had grown, and society was stratified into scholars (*ulama*), army (*mujahid*), governors, and citizens. This social change coupled with the emergence of intense contentions in the fields of philosophy and *kalam*, pushed some people into seriously considering abandoning this world and practicing asceticism. Though the organizational abandonment of worldly life generated a bountiful form of spiritual life to develop, this style of life style was not practiced during the time of the Companions. As his predecessors, Gülen interpreted the abandonment of the world as to "abandon in the heart, not in practice."[19] This interpretation has brought his understanding of asceticism (*zuhd*) closer to the Companions. In his first speeches, sermons, and articles, Gülen often made references to the *zuhd* of the Companions, emphasizing their piety, profundity in worship and obedience, and their zeal and devotion in conveying the religion. In hundreds of occasions, he emphasized central Sufi concepts like asceticism (*zuhd*), piety (*taqwa*), abstinence (*wara*), heart (*qalb*), carnal self (*nafs*), fear (*khawf*), knowledge of God (*marifa*), love (*mahabba*) . . . All of these Sufi tunes emerged as personal religious transcendence and personal living. He has never turned Sufism into a social phenomenon. Instead, he placed more emphasis on the social existence and collective personality (*şahs-ı manevi*) of the community. The community mission he meticulously stressed was comprised of religious and social elements including spreading the word of God, sacrifice, devotion to Almighty, service to the people. Again, for this he interpreted differently some principles of classical Sufism, terms such as seclusion (*uzlat*) and privacy (*halwat*), which together strive to isolate individuals from the society. Gülen's brand of asceticism perceived seclusion and privacy as personal, and at the same time, he focused on the benefits of sympathizing with the troubles and sorrows of other people in society.[20] In brief, Gülen stresses Sufi profundity and terminology in personal meaning. Socially, he advocates communal activity, collective body, and service to the Almighty and to people in a systematic format. This actually complies with the religious conduct ascribed to the Prophet, peace be upon him, and to his Companions and the way they conveyed the message of Islam. They lived under extremely dire conditions, but they always manifested utmost care in their conduct, and they were by no means behind later Sufis in spiritual excellence and profundity. Unlike those early Sufis, the initial community of the Prophet never adopted notions of seclusion or privacy away from society. They preferred to strive for God and to convey His message. Gülen's communal activity and central mission emerges from this tradition.

Surely there have been many movements, communities, and formations that have accepted Sufi lifestyle in their ways of personal manner and social action. It is not our project to generate an opinion about their manners and opinions here. Rather, our goal has been to point out that Sufism has existed in different modes in the history of Islamic spirituality.

Here it is appropriate to touch upon another point. *Tariqa* has another wider meaning. Spiritual life, that is, the life one experiences on his walk to God, in whatever form, is called *tariqa*. This devotion does not have to comply with any Sufi order. *Tariqa*, in this meaning, is personal. For every person who set off the path to God has a personal life as experienced in a spiritual world. Early Sufis state that "paths (*tariqs*) to God count to the number of initiates."[21]

This definition of *tariqa* is more valid for the second and pre-second century Sufi life. After the second century, however, *tariqa* attained an organizational structure with a particular terminology, form of teaching and ceremony, rules and methods. It ceased to be solely a spiritual ascetic experience of devotion to God. Although it has not been unanimously agreed neither as a social phenomenon, nor cognitively, many consider Sufism to be different than *tariqa*. If we are to acknowledge this difference, then we can place Gülen's understanding closer to Sufism rather than to *tariqa*. Nevertheless, today's *tariqa* forms are widely differentiated as compared to those of the third and fourth century. Modern *tariqa*s, along with retaining Sufi understanding based upon personal spiritual and moral experience, expanded their understanding of service to the social sphere. This massive spiritual and social transformation in our time should not be ignored, as well.

In this regard, today's *tariqa* converge with "community" forms. Seclusion, privacy, and abandonment-based asceticism have widely diverged from classical *tariqa* forms. However, formally traditional methods and ceremonies are being preserved. Several modern rituals and symbols have been added to older methods and principles.

Despite such discrepancies, however, many define their existence as "*tariqa*."

While Gülen can be considered a modern Sufi, the movement or community inspired by him cannot be characterized as a formal Sufi movement or *tariqa*. It does not identify with a particular Sufi or *tariqa* tradition by way of rules, methods, or hierarchical structure. As already mentioned, Gülen admits that Sufi terminology, in general, are necessary for the development of one's personal aptitude. Beyond this, he emphasizes the significance of these concepts in guiding Muslims' social life. However, he does not postulate a *tariqa* organization as a social movement. For these obvious reasons, defining his movement as a *tariqa* contradicts with both historical realities and basic dynamics of the movement.

COMMUNITY AND THE CONCEPT OF "COLLECTIVE PERSONALITY"

Above already stated, Sufism is present in the Gülen movement, not in the form of a *tariqa*, but in individual practices, and their emphasis is more on the collective personality, or *şahs-ı manevi*. This emphasis acknowledges the community to be a corporate body that shares spiritual unity and personality. This body is a collective representation of a unified system of will power, idea, beliefs, and behaviors. Communal principles emerge as concrete forms of these unifying wills and efforts. Like a piece of ice melting in the ocean and thus becoming the ocean, every person degrades his ego to become one with the collective spiritual personality. Partaking in this spiritual unity means that one should leave behind, or at least not give priority to, his or her personal interests, pleasures, and engagements. This happens primarily in areas where the community expects action from its participants.

The formation of a collective personality shapes around the principle of spreading the word of God. All communal activities, rituals, values, principles, and goals intend for this aim. The ideal of spreading the word of God to all of humankind require the efforts of both single individuals and the collective body of the community. In all cooperative forms, even in ideological and political organizations, parties are believed to have a metaphysical and/ or a mystical essence. Followers or members are expected to be respectful to this essence and to disregard their personal interests. Yet these types of entities are shaped upon concrete benefits, expectations, and worldly ideals. They do not seek God's approval, nor do they focus on the idea of eternity and the hereafter. They exist on the foundations of attaining power, seeking a post, or searching for fame in a direction that would enable them to apply political or social pressure on societal balance. One should not confuse the spiritual personality of the community with organizations shaped around worldly, material aims.

On the other hand, it is believed that collective personality is naturally blessed with God's benevolence and favor. In the Sufi tradition, initiates receive divine favors through spiritual experience and practice. In the case of the collective spiritual personality of a community, divine favors are always greater when compared to favors to persons and personal experiences. The Prophet says that God's consent and good pleasure is always with the community manifested in the form óf favors and blessings.[22] At this point, I would like to mention a traditional Sufi view, which is considered to be in the realm of subjective knowledge, in order to make a contribution to the comprehension of collective spiritual personality. In Sufi literature, prominent spiritual people are known as *qutb, qutb al-aktab, ghaws* etc. They are imagined as central power transformers who transfer divine favors and spiritual prosperity to followers. Divine favors and divine benevolence is first directed to these people, and then they re-distribute and transport this revenue to others in accordance to their closeness with God. This phenomenon in the Sufi tradition is represented by the collective spiritual personality in the context of the community. These historical spiritual personalities exist today in the form of communities. The unity and corporate body of community, and its spiritual presence hold a spiritual and metaphysical meaning:

> Devotion to a collective personality means dissolving in the community and unifying with it. Community is a group of people who gathered around same thought and ideal. . . . Being a community can only be attained by reaching collective consciousness. The collective consciousness dissolves the individual in its multidimensional composition, making it yet another of its dimensions; then no absolute individual remains. The individual is communalized, and the community turns to a single individual. . . . Prayers observed in this community entirely flow to the same pool. Collective personality of the community rapidly soars to higher spiritual ranks. . . . This rise continues, as long as the community preserves its qualitative essence, to such pinnacles that sometimes a community represents the highest spiritual rank. . . . When a community ascends to this rank the capacity of spiritual fulfillment both in this world and the hereafter widens in the same proportion and sometimes comprises al members of the community.[23]

As we have seen, Gülen attaches importance to the collective personality of the community. For him, the collective personality serves as a means that makes communal activities bountiful, and adds to their spiritual value. Further, he stresses that spiritual ascension and journey through collective personality is more reliable, less risky, and away from arrogance than by way of other methods. This journey is toward sainthood, or *walaya* as it is called in Sufism, but in this case it is the sainthood of the collective personality:

> Representation of *walaya* by the "collective personality" is the most straight and guaranteed path. For, there is no circumstance that may lead the initiate to feel conceited. The post attained belongs to the collective personality; the individual is protected from any obstacles and handicaps that may drag that person to arrogance. ... On the other hand, today no one can attain such spiritual ranks relying on one's own efforts. Yet we can attain peaks only by affiliating to the collective personality . . .[24]

Gülen talks about three pre-conditions a community needs to meet in order to represent the highest spiritual rank:

1. Community members should be tightly linked to each other,
2. Everybody must fully share the same feelings,
3. They must pay utmost care about observing prayers, remembrance, and all types of servanthood.[25]

Sharing the same feelings, spiritual fellowship, observing prayers, being watchful of divine decrees and prohibitions are all introduced as components that form and reinforce the collective personality of a community. Unity of feelings, thoughts, and ideals lays the foundation of a community, and it is essential for its existence. As with all communities, common principles shared by everybody comprise the tangible foundations of a community. The formation of a collective personality, however, requires a sort of glue that takes its form in a spiritual lifestyle based on sincere belief practiced by its participants. Without this paste, the collective personality of the community may be exposed to weakening, disintegration, and dispersion. Every single person should comprehend that being attached to the community means also being a member of a spiritual cooperation: "Every person attached to a Muslim community is also accepted as a member of a spiritual cooperation. Thus his or her every action possesses all advantages of being a member to this kind of cooperation. An individual, by his or her position, shares all rewards granted to the community . . ."[26]

Here the concept of "collective personality" appears as a Sufi-based concept. Although there are people in the Sufi tradition that underline this concept, this is not a common situation. The concept achieved generality and profundity in the modern period, at the time when modern communities emerged. In fact, we have enough social material to engage in an intellectual analysis of the concept as it might be viewed within the parameters of a modern paradigm. The framework of definition referred by terms like "corporate body" and "institutional identity" is useful to understand "collective personality." We relate a corporate body to a social rule or a legal concept, and thus we reach a conceptualization about it. Collective personality represents roughly the same thing. In modern law, the concept of "legal personality" falls into the field of personal rights.

The concept of the collective personality has become more relevant today with the formation of communities in modern times. It is also one of the most central concepts of Sufism, for one of the main aims of Sufism is to elevate people to the rank of *walaya* by training and purifying the self. This rank can be attained in the widest sense through the collective personality of communities. The journey of the collective personality toward *walaya* is relevant with the collective presence of the community as much as it is with each and every individual member. By engaging in collective personality, members in a community can obtain spiritual revenue with more intensity and greater velocity than can be obtained by individual practices as in traditional Sufism. Therefore, in the context of the modern community, the concepts of "collective personality" and "*walaya*" are wide and deep enough to encapsulate the entire lexicon of traditional Sufi terminology.

Community is regarded as the recipient of every kind of blessing. In a community, each word, practice, and feeling of service are made bountiful, and it serves as the transporter of people's spiritual journey and *walaya*. Community functions like a spiritual cooperation. As well as increasing feelings of partnership, company, and devotion, it functions as a moral paste that bonds society.

The term "collective personality" is not an imaginative concept used solely to express the institutional structure of community. The Earth, heaven, the stars, the mountains etc. are all believed in Sufi terminology to have spiritual personalities. One interpretation of Islamic cosmology contends that the basis for this reality is rooted in the Qur'anic verse, "*whatever is in the heavens and the earth glorifies God through their disposition.*"[27] Some prophetic sayings mention angels with forty thousand (or even a hundred thousand) heads and mouths that are all used to praise God. Such angels carry all remembrances and praises of the stars, the moon, the mountains etc. to God. A mountain and a tree have a spiritual personality that is watched by an appointed angel (*malak-i muak-kal*). If a mountain with hundred thousand trees has a spiritual personality, then certainly a community with hundred thousand members would have a spiritual personality. This matter is not only epistemological and interpretational; it connects directly to the Muslim perception of humanity, existence, and the universe.

The aforementioned Prophetic saying reads, "God's hand (of might), power, favor and benevolence are on the community." On Earth, the point that the God looks upon is the perfect person, *insan al-kamil*. The most comprehensive manifestation of God's favor and benevolence is directed towards the perfect person. The "perfect person" represents the ideal model of humanity, sought by Sufi throughout the history of Islam. The purpose of all spiritual and moral struggles is to become a "perfect person." That said, when compared to a community, a "perfect person" can not reach the same level of God's favors and benevolence. A genius person can not match the performance and accuracy of a committee of scientists; likewise a person's spiritual performance can not reach that of a community. The most abundant and comprehensive manifestation of God's mercy, favor, and abundance are gifted to the collective spiritual personality of the community. Therefore, the community and collective personality have become two of the most important elements in the Muslim tradition and in activities of spreading the message of Islam in modern times.[28]

BASIC DYNAMICS OF THE MOVEMENT

Analyzing the internal dynamics of a movement is important for two reasons. First, it allows others to perceive the structure by which the movement is organized. Second, it prevents others from falling into the trap of overlooking the totality of the movement, as they focus on partial analyses. I use dynamics here to mean the key concepts of the movement. Intellectual and social attitudes of a movement are shaped by the movement's dynamics. Social science analyses that study a movement proceed on safer grounds if they are aware of that movement's dynamics, and they do not fall into frequent fallacies. Understanding a movement's dynamics allows us to pinpoint who is making an objective analysis, and who forges a "pirated" analysis without any knowledge. For instance, a person who strives to comply with the basic dynamics of Islamic Sufi practice by being humble in his or her relations with others (*tawadhu*), or regarding himself as inferior to others (*mahwiyat*), would surely appear as a shy person. An observer, who is unaware of any Sufi and ascetic dynamics, might interpret this humble attitude as hypocritical or clandestine. If an analysis does not account for this movement's Muslim Sufi dynamics and experiences, can we really call this analysis "scientific"?

Sufi, moral, and spiritual profundity in Islam invites believers to be humble and tolerant in their family and their social relations. Personal virtue and social maturity are pre-requisites. Thus, in order to understand this movement, it is first necessary to understand the spiritual dynamics of Islam, and the extent to which Islam influences its participants. It is almost impossible to analyze even an ordinary Muslim's intellectual and social life without first understanding the profound nature of Islam in general. Cultural Islam gives us a general outlook in regard to the theological, mental, moral, and social relations of Muslims. When we look from the window of general dynamics, we can obtain a first glimpse of the individual, spiritual, moral, and social attitudes of Muslims in a community. From all these points of view, elaborating on the religious/spiritual, social, and cultural dynamics of the Gülen movement would help us formulate a proper rendering of the religious and socio-cultural attitudes of the movement in general.

Indeed, the titles and concepts that I will highlight are also important in regard to how they are interpreted and how they are transferred to social practice, as well as to their deep meaning in
Muslim cultural perception. The importance of Gülen comes from
his success in transforming these dynamics into action in socio-cultural life. In theory, these cultural and religious dynamics existed
in books and other sources for almost 1,500 years.

The most distinctive characteristic of these dynamics is that
they exist in parallel to "eternity," a notion to which Islam is naturally directed as a divine revelation and religion. Islam undertakes
the task of helping people reach eternal and absolute reality by
showing them how to pass beyond the relative and transient world
of creation. This pace towards eternity is immanent in the essence
of all the internal and social dynamics of the Gülen movement. In
fact, this ideal exists in the essence of almost all religions. Yet this
ideal in the Gülen movement is not solely abstract. It has become
an active program that has encompassed almost all internal and
social relations. Gülen's human model entails embracing selfless
service and altruism with motivations that extend toward eternity.[29] The ideal of eternity broadens the meaning and importance
of all other dynamics. This principle is regenerated as a basic
dynamic again and again, in every act and attempt, which means
that faith is revived in almost every social relation and service.

The topics of focus here comprise the basic dynamics that por-
tray the general outlook of this movement. Some of the titles may
not be fully representative of the movement, for they might have
been produced due to material, social, or particular conditions over
the 30-year course of the movement's development. Gülen's rendering of these dynamics is also worth attention. As in his general
Islamic attitude and in his general perception, Gülen can be considered to have a conservative aptitude regarding the movement's
dynamics. Yet, commenting on the same dynamics in different times
and places, he broadens their meaning and thus creates a self-gener-

ating and self-producing system. This wide spectrum of intellectual, philosophical, and literal resources renovates the substance of his discourse without affecting its basic characteristics. Here we will briefly touch upon some of the basic dynamics of the movement. Understanding the diversity of form, meaning, and style which these dynamics have assumed in different times and places would require a more comprehensive analysis of his works and a closer observation of his social activities.

a. *Magnanimity*

While magnanimity (*vicdan genişliği*[30]) may not exist as an internal dynamic in the Gülen movement, it certainly has a decisive role in interpreting other dynamics. Since the 1970s, in his writings and speeches, Gülen has charged this concept with a broad meaning, even though he has allusively referred to it without much stress. Magnanimity has a very special status in his system of thinking, belief, and action. In this way, Gülen looks at all manifestations of moral, individual, and social life from a magnanimous perspective.

Magnanimity covers all intrinsic experience and knowledge of faith, while practically being in the social and ethical realm of existence. By this concept, Gülen seems to refer to a mature, sincere piety and integrity on the one hand, and he emphasizes a virtuous society comprised of people with a high quality of wisdom and knowledge of God on the other. In his discourse, the concept expands from the spiritual/moral depths of individuals to the endlessness realms of social existence. Gülen also considers this concept as the only touchstone of goodness, refinement, and reality. He considers this concept to be a criterion against which all thoughts, actions, and social projects should be evaluated to find out whether they can really bring a benefit and favor to all of humanity. Gülen states that one cannot speak of revival or renaissance within a given society if that society is unaware of this reality.[31]

b. Communicating the word of God (call, conveyance, and guidance)

Over the course of Muslim history, *i'lay-i kelimetullah*, communicating the word of God, has been a matter of discussion in individual, social, and political contexts. Excluding those interpretations designed according to social or temporal conditions, this concept covers three dimensions in its broadest sense: the call to faith, conveying the message, and guidance. In Gülen's discourse, communicating the name of God includes all three dimensions. He integrates each with human existence in this world. The purpose of existence in this world is to exalt God's name and word.

The association of physical *jihad* with *i'lay-i kelimetullah* is being exploited and misrepresented in current Western analyses. Such discourses often equate Islam with war, violence, and terror. Gülen has a separate work in which he extensively explains this concept.[32] We suggest that when scholars seek to analyze the basic dynamics by which Muslims exalt God, they should consult this work for an in-depth, internal perspective. In this work, readers will find that Gülen assigns a cosmic meaning to this concept to explain the human existence in this world.

c. Living for others

Gülen attaches importance to this principle of "living for others" (*yaşatma ideali*) such that he interprets it as a basic dynamic that would make a nation awaken. Every society must make sacrifices. Sacrifice is beyond and above worldly gain, and thus its definition exceeds that of mere altruism. On the contrary, it is more akin to idealistic heroism. Such altruism constitutes the character of people who are uninterested in personal or worldly gain, and who are committed to God's favor. Gülen describes these types of people as "architects of soul" and as "physicians of thought." These are people who are able to instill in the society a consciousness of responsibility and concern for others. Without physicians of soul, it is not possible to preserve the established values that pertain to the Islamic civilization and that have formed its historical identity. If such preservation is not possible, any hope of instigating a renaissance and revival of this civilization and identity will be lost. Such people are an important dynamic, according to Gülen:

> Today, what we need are brave people who selflessly work in the service of God and who wave aside personal benefits and egoism . . . who writhe with people's miseries . . . who have a torch of knowledge in their hands, and who fight the ignorance and rudeness that ignites tinder everywhere . . . who, with eminent belief and determination, come to the rescue of those stranded . . . like stallions, hold on their course without repelling and without griming . . . those who ramp with pleasure of living for others while forgetting the desire of living.[33]
>
> I believe that all humanity will be pleased, and that the centuries-long miseries of suffering people, will come to an end, and that the world will once again will come to an axis of thanks in regard to the ideals that related his salvation with rescuing others. Such people can trample on their future and prosperity in the name of others' happiness; they can circulate in the veins of others like blood; they can splash over yearning and thirsts and breathe life everywhere. They then can bind their actions to the responsibility that is idealized in the depths of their inner selves. With compassion that transcends personal responsibility, and through kindness that could encompass all humanity, they will try to bring for us the spirit and significance that we have lost; they will remind us of our human significance. Meanwhile, they will constitute a model for perplexed souls who have lived without ideals for such a long time.[34]
>
> Our society needs only heroes of ideals: those who can reach out to help first our nation, and then all humanity, with the feeling of compassion; and every time they raise their hand to God, they pray for others. As such a great requirement could not be met by others, it falls upon us who start from ourselves to articulate it.[35]
>
> We consider living for ourselves as egoism, and we have found such a consideration revolting. It has been our passion to live for others and to prepare them for eternal happiness.

Even if it were possible to return to life, even if we were free to choose the alternatives of this new life, we would certainly choose to "live for others" again, we would certainly dedicate ourselves to humanity, and we would prepare humankind for resurrection. We would not mind any misprision . . . We would not be deterred by cries of reaction . . . We would not quarrel with anybody who has accused us with false and malicious accusations . . . We would smile while weeping inside.[36]

The ideal people burn like candles despite themselves, and they illuminate others . . .[37]

A true friend who is a mature person is the one who can utter "after you," even while exiting from Hell and entering Paradise.[38]

What we are always stressing is that it is those who live their lives in sincerity, loyalty, and altruism at the expense of their own selves in order to make others live who are the true inheritors of the historical dynamics to whom we can entrust our souls. They do not ever desire that the masses follow them. Yet their existence is such a powerful, inevitable invitation that all run to them, wherever they are, as if these devout people were a centre of attraction.[39]

Individual projects of enlightenment that are not planned to aid the community are doomed to fruitlessness. Moreover, it is not possible to revive values that have been destroyed in the hearts of the individual in society, nor in the conscience, nor in the will power. Just as plans and projects for individual salvation that are independent of the salvation of others are nothing more than an illusion, so, too, the thought of achieving success as a whole by paralyzing the individual awakening is a fantasy.

Living for others is the most important factor that determines the behavior of such heroes. Their greatest worry is their quest for eligibility for such missions, whereas their most prevalent characteristic is that their utmost ambition is their search for God's consent. When striving to enlighten others, they feel no pain nor do they undergo any shock caused by the delight of enlightening others. The achievements that such people accomplish are regarded as revelations of His holy aid, and such people bow in modesty, nullifying themselves again and again, every day. In addition to all this, they tremble at the idea that their emotions are bound to interfere with the works that they have caused to come into existence, and groan; "You are all I need."[40]

Expecting nothing in return is the rose of our land. Altruism is the lotus of our gardens. It is our lot to attain but not to enjoy. We forget living for ourselves while burning with the desire of living for others. It is our people who know how to be in the front while serving, and how to stay behind in compensation. The world has discovered from us to love unconditionally.[41]

Perfect believers do not stick only to their personal development or perfection; they are determined almost like prophets to open themselves up for everyone and to embrace each and every person. They devote their lives to the happiness of others both in this world as well as in the hereafter, at the expense of neglecting themselves. They live like the Companions of the Prophet; they walk in a direction opposite to where their carnal selves urge, and they spread light all around, for they have that potential to illuminate in their essence like a candle. They are always on alert for darkness, and they struggle to keep it at bay . . . As they burn all the time, they are hurt inside; nevertheless, neither constant burning nor extermination can restrain them from enlightening others.[42]

We are not in need of local or foreign grants, favors or ideologies. We need the physicians of thought and spirit who can arouse in all people the consciousness of the value of responsibility, sacrifice, and suffering for others; who can produce mental and spiritual depth and sincerity in the place of promises of passing happiness; who can, with a single attempt, make us reach the point of observing the beginning and the end of creation.

Now we are waiting, looking forward to the arrival of these people, who have so much love for their responsibility and cause that, if necessary, they would even give up entering Paradise; people like this, if they have already entered, would then seek ways of leaving Paradise. Like Muhammad, the Messenger of God, who said, "If they placed the sun in my right and the moon in my left to abandon my cause, I would not until God made the truth prevail or I died in the attempt." This is the horizon of God's Messenger. Bediüzzaman Said Nursi, a scholar exuberant with the rays that emanate from God's Messenger, bent double by the pain of his cause said, "In my eyes I have neither love for Paradise nor fear for Hell, and if I saw the faith of my people secure, I would be ready now to be burned in hell-fire." Likewise, Abu Bakr opened his hands and prayed in a way that would shake the heavens, "O my Lord, make my body so great that I alone fill up Hell and thus no place may be left for anyone else."

Humanity is terribly in need of people with inner depths and sincerity now, more than anything else, for people who suffer and cry for the sins and errors of others; who look forward to forgiveness and pardon of others before their own; who, instead of entering Paradise and taking their pleasures individually there, prefer to stay in the A'raf (between the Paradise and Hell) and from there, try to take all the people to Paradise along with them; and who, even if they enter Paradise, will not be able find time to enjoy the pleasures of Paradise because of their thoughts for others, and their concern to save them from the hell-fire.[43]

d. The spirit of devotion

This principle should be viewed as a continuation of the previous discussion in regard to the level of moral dynamic ascribed to "living for others," whereby individuals devote themselves to God and to other people. Let us elaborate. As we know, the origin of love, in all its forms, emanates from the Almighty Creator. All loves and affections, as well as all delights and beauties, are the manifestations of His beautiful names. The same manifestation is best expressed in the famous Turkish couplet, "Loving all creatures by reason of the Creator" (*yaratığı severiz, Yaratan da ötürü*) by Yunus and celebrated in the West as Muslim humanism. This is such a great manifestation that it compasses all fields of human existence and relations. This phrase is the most concise "humanist" message of Islam. It could be said that for Gülen, this principle is kept alive and reproduced within the very spirit of devotion. When we comprehend the notions of "Creator and created," we will catch the basic characteristics of Muslim affection as distinguished from philosophic humanism that has no relation with the divine. For in Islam, in the origin of all loves is the reality of the Creator.[44] If it were not for the manifestation of His beautiful names and attributes, humanity would be deprived of affection, compassion, and kindness. According to Islam, therefore, people should dedicate all love and affection to the Creator before all else. Without this focus, one cannot devote one's love or affection to another person by way of giving up one's own pleasures. The spirit and feeling of devotion to God, therefore, bestows the basic motivation for serving humanity. The spirit of devotion produces a moral dynamic that electrifies all love, every relation, every sacrifice, and every service therein:

> The most remarkable feature of those who have devoted themselves to the bestowal of God's consent and to the ideal of loving and being loved by Him is that they never expect anything—material or spiritual—in return. Things like profit, wealth, cost, comfort, etc., things to which people of this world pay great attention, do not mean much; they hold no value, nor are they considered as criteria.
>
> To devotees, the value of their ideals transcends that of the earthly ones to such an extent that it is almost impossible to divert them from what they seek—God's gratuitous consent—and lead them to any other ideal. In fact, stripped entirely of finite and transient things, devotees undergo such a transformation in their hearts to turn to God that they are changed because they recognize no goal other than their ideal. Since they devote themselves completely to making people love God and to being loved by God, dedicating their lives to enlightening others—and, once again, because they have managed to orient their goal in this unified direction, which in a sense contributes to the value of this ideal—they avoid divisive and antagonist thoughts, such as "they" and "we," "others," and "ours." Neither do such people have any problems—explicit or concealed—with other people. In contrast, all they think of is how they can be useful to society and how they can avoid disputes with the society of which they are members. When they detect a problem in society, they take action, like a spiritual leader rather than a warrior, leading people to virtue and lofty spirituality, abstaining from any sort of political dominance or thought of rule.

What composes the depths of these devoted spirits is knowledge, the use of this knowledge, a strong and sound understanding of morality and its application in every aspect of life, faithful virtue and the awareness of its indispensability, among other factors. They seek refuge in God from fame and interest-based cold propaganda and ostentatious acts and deeds, things which indeed do not promise anything in the name of their future—that is, for their afterlife. Furthermore, living in accordance with their principles, they ceaselessly endeavor to lead those who watch and imitate to be in awe of sublime human values. Doing all this, such people do not ever expect any interest or kindness from anyone, and they try hard to evade any kind of personal interest or profit; they avoid this as they would a snake or a scorpion. After all, their inner richness has a centripetal power that does not allow any acts of advertisement, boasting, or ostentation. Their amiable behavior, also a reflection of their spirits, is of such a quality that it fascinates and makes discerning people follow them.

For this very reason, these devotees never desire to boast about themselves or to advertise or spread propaganda about themselves, nor are they ambitious to be well-known or appreciated. . . .

Devotees do not experience emptiness in their mental lives and reasoning thanks to this understanding of a unified direction. On the contrary, they remain open to reason, science and logic, regarding this as a prerequisite for their beliefs. Having been melted in the depths of closeness to God, a closeness which depends on one's merit, and in the ocean that is like divine unity, their earthly desires and corporeal passion take on a new shape (spiritual enjoyment as a result of God's consent) with a new pattern, a new style. Thus, devotees can breathe the same air as the angels at the peaks of spiritual life while conversing with terrestrial ones, fulfilling the licit requirements of life on Earth. For this reason, these devotees are considered as being related to both the present and the future worlds. Their relation with the present world is due to the fact that they apply and comply with physical forces. What ties them to the next world is the fact that they evaluate every matter in the light of their spiritual life and that of the heart. Any inhibitions in the worldly life that are imposed by the spiritual life do not necessarily entail a complete abandonment of the worldly life;

it is for this reason that these people cannot entirely despise the world. In contrast, they always stand in the center rather than on the periphery of the world and rule it. This stance, however, is not one for, or in, the name of the world, but rather one in the name of complying with physical forces and an attempt to connect everything to the Hereafter.

As a matter of fact, this is the way to keep the body in its own frame and the spirit on its own horizon; it is the way to lead life under the leadership of the heart and the spirit. The finite and restricted corporeal life must be to the extent that corporeality deserves, while the spiritual life, always open to eternity, must seek infinitude. If one thinks only supreme and transcendent thoughts, if one leads a life as the Life-Giver demands, if one regards illuminating others as the fundamental of one's life, and if one always seeks the zenith, then one naturally becomes a practitioner of a supreme program, and, thus, to a certain extent, one limits personal desires and passions. . . .

Provided this devotion is wholehearted and sincere, it is always likely that God will bestow His blessings onto these kinds of people. The more that people aim to please God, and the more wholeheartedly that they are attached to God, the more likely they are to be appreciated and rewarded, and the more likely it is that they will become the subject of supreme conversations. The every thought, word and act of such people will become a luminous atmosphere in the next world, an atmosphere which can also be called "the smiling face of fate." Such fortunate people, who filled their sails with the white winds of their fortune, sail with special blessing toward Him, not attaching themselves elsewhere. What the Qur'an presents as a depiction of these people is worth seeing:

> *Men (of great distinction) whom neither commerce nor exchange (nor any other worldly preoccupations) can divert from the remembrance of God, and establishing the Prayer in conformity with all its conditions, and paying the Prescribed Purifying Alms; they are in fear of a Day on which all hearts and eyes will be overturned. God will reward them in accordance with the best of what they have ever done, and give them yet more out of His bounty (i.e. more than they deserve). God provides beyond all measure for whom He wills.* (Nur 24:37-38)[45]

e. Sacrifice, fidelity, and loyalty

One of the most remarkable dynamics of the Gülen movement centers on sacrifice (*fedakarlık*) and fidelity (*sadakat*). These concepts are obviously not particular to this movement. There has always been a common emphasis on these concepts in the Muslim tradition. As we tried to emphasize in previous sections, the reason we include them as core concepts for the Gülen movement is that Gülen himself defines these characteristics with a deep sense of profundity and with rich and layered meaning. He has motivated peoples' sensations to the extent that he has generated a new system and campaign of sacrifice. When we speak of sacrifice or fidelity in the Gülen movement, we do not simply speak of solidarity and helping. Gülen prescribes, as in other criteria of piety, an open-ended sense of sacrifice that reaches for the extreme limits of human and moral senses. When the issue is piety or service of humanity, he is never satisfied with normal limits. He longs to amplify human beneficence, loyalty, and fidelity. Because of this, Gülen often refers to the metaphors of, "a horse that runs until his/her heart bursts," and "a winged turtle-dove." The horse in his system symbolizes the heroes of love who hurry by day and night to their service; the turtle-dove symbolizes high and eminent ideals. From here, we may discover that his heroes are each idealistic people:

> Sacrifice is one of the important characteristics of a person who teaches others. Those who do not, or cannot, risk sacrifice from the start can never be a person of cause. People who do not have a cause cannot be successful. Yes, those who are ready to leave at one stretch whenever necessary, their wealth, life, family, position, fame, etc., things which many people desire and put as the purpose of life—that their cause eventually reaches the peaks is certain and inevitable.
>
> Thus, the Prophet, peace be upon him, instilled, starting from himself and then from his close circle, the spirit of sacrifice. He practiced and demonstrated this throughout his life to all people who have devoted themselves to his cause. For instance, Khadija, may God be pleased with her, spent every-

thing she had for the sake of this sacred cause, even without the Prophet, her husband, asking. She covered all the expenses for banquets offered to Meccan pagans in order to convey the message of Islam to them. Being once one of the richest people of pre-Islamic Mecca, this renowned woman had not even the wealth to buy her burial shroud when she died.

In addition to expending their wealth for people of cause, the emigration to another place—i.e., leaving behind their home when required, leaving all that they know in order to be able to practice their religion, thought, freedom, and humanity—is a sacrificial act in search of God's favor. For example, Abu Bakr, Umar, Uthman, and Ali (may God be pleased with them), rich and poor, young and old, men and women—almost all of them emigrated at one point or another. While emigrating from their homeland, they left all their wealth to the cruel and oppressive people of Mecca, and they only took enough food to suffice them during journey. Yes, while emigrants (*Muhajirun*) sacrificed in order to convey and represent their cause, they sincerely believed and devoted themselves to God's will. In return, the helpers (*Ansar*) in Medina showed great sacrifice by welcoming and embracing them. Yes, the Ansar welcomed their Meccan brothers and sisters, though they were poor and earned their living from farming only; they behaved in an extraordinarily noble manner.

Today's people who communicate faith and guidance should perform in the same way by practicing the sacrifice represented by the Companions of the Prophet, who once fashioned a zenith society in almost every field of life. Otherwise, . . . these people cannot succeed in communicating the faith.[46]

Loyalty (*vefa*) is one of the roses grown in a friendly environment. It is uncommon and even impossible to see loyalty in an atmosphere of enmity. The peaceful breeze of loyalty blows around those who share the same things in feeling, thought, and imagination. Enmity, hatred, and jealousy do not give loyalty an instant to take a breath. In an environment of love and generosity, loyalty grows, whereas in an environment of hatred, loyalty diminishes.

Some define fidelity as the integration of the human being with his or her soul. This is appropriate, though incomplete. The truth is that it is very hard to speak of loyalty in regard to those who have no spiritual life. Talking the truth, and keeping one's word or oath, is connected with one's spiritual profundity. Hypocrites cannot save themselves from lying and deceptions; they violate their own word and they are never serious about the responsibilities they have undertaken. Expecting loyalty from people who are deprived of a soulful dimension illustrates unawareness and naiveté.

Whoever trusts someone without loyalty becomes wretched. Whoever sets off on a journey with them gets stranded. Whoever respects him as a guide grieves all the time:

> *Hoping for loyalty from him*
> *Filled my eyes with grief*
> *And left one foot cureless . . .*

A person deserves trust and ascends through loyalty. If a home is built on loyalty, then it keeps on standing and becomes lively. A nation would attain virtues with this noble sense. A state maintains its reputation only with this sense in the eyes of its citizens. If loyalty is lost in a country, it is unlikely to talk of a mature person, or a home that promises security, or a stabilized and reliable state. In such a country, people are suspicious against each other; homes are troubled; the state is inauspicious to its citizens; and everything is alien to the other, even though they happen to be aligned next to one another.[47]

f. Representing and communicating the faith

Today, there are numerous political, philosophical, and ideological schools of thought and movements, and each of them vocalizes some grand cause that they claim to have inherited from the past. Among them, there are some that, although their discourse includes useful things for humanity, amount to little more than glorified slogans. They do not bother referring to any criteria or social reality to ascertain whether their thoughts are feasible or not, and whether they are uttered by true representatives. Despite this, any idea, thought, or movement has theoretical and practical aspects. Practical feasibility is as important as the idea and theory itself. At this point, the people who carry these ideas into practice come into question. Their merit and ability to represent the theory determine that movement's success. Representation (*temsil*) comprises the feasibility of opinions and ideas as it relates to the credibility of their holders. No movement can be successful without having sufficient people who can represent its cause. The fact that the degree of success can change in accordance to some criteria does not affect validity of this fact.

Gülen has emphasized this fact of representation since his early years. Full of sincerity, excitement, and action, he quoted passages from the lives of Prophets and the lives of their followers, to highlight the necessity of turning thought into action. In his retelling of their stories, their distinctive personalities, their patience, their endurance, and their sincerity, Gülen highlighted the importance of this principle as being primary in the mobilization of the movement. To him, if you do not have the ability to represent, society will not take your cause seriously and you will have nothing to say to the society. Gülen interprets this principle as internal-external integrity:

> Those who want to reform the world must first reform themselves. If they want to lead others to a better world, they must purify their inner worlds of hatred, rancor, and jealousy, and adorn their outer worlds with virtue. The words of those who cannot control and discipline themselves, and who have not refined their feelings, may seem attractive and insightful at first. However, even if they somehow manage to inspire others, which they sometimes do, the sentiments they arouse will soon wither.[48]

> When hearts do not lend an ear to Islam carefully, it does not make its voice heard; if the spoken words are not represented in conduct, then its voice is turned down and it does not inspire anything in hearts. Words not only spoken but also conducted instill thrill in hearts and attain all aptitudes beyond all distances.[49]

> Believers must believe very sincerely in the heart; they must behave as if they see God at every instant and feel the reverence of being observed by Him. For real believers, their conduct must suffice for telling about their faith to other people and convincing them; there should be no need for them to design mind stretchers. Their sleep, speech, glance, and posture must

suffice. People who see them must be able to tell that "this earnest human being may not behave in frivolity; this harmless face may not lie." One of the major problems today is the inability to strike an attitude like this, leading to the failure to act out of internal maturity both individually and socially."[50]

The great magic of Jesus' apostles was their sincerity and the credibility of their manners. The most important reason the friends of the last Prophet managed to convey the light of faith to the entire world, and why they found friendly reception, was their Muslim manner. Centuries later, students of the Bediüzzaman exemplified similar sincerity and cordiality in a way as if they could see God (ihsan). In our time, however, Muslims have expanded in quantity; but they have lost much of Islam's inner spirit. While we possess reason and logic, and while science and technology is more advanced than in our ancestors' time, we do not have the same heart they bore. We are deprived of the real favor of feeling God in every heartbeat. Our heartbeats should have a manifestation on the outside, like a clock which has an inner mechanism that is simultaneously transferred to action on the hands outside every second. The real center of life is the heart.[51]

Gülen attributes the chronic social posture of the Muslim world to a deficiency in representation:

> The deficiency of the Muslim world is not in science, technology, or richness. I have to admit that these all have some influence; however, the primary reason behind our deficiency is conduct and the immense quality of heart that should direct all our actions. Our deficiency is with regards to a Muslim-like image. Because of this deficiency, we do not have people today like Sadreddin Konevi, Rumi, Naqshiband, Hasan Shadhili, Ahmad Badawi, Imam Rabbani, Mevlana Halid, or Bediüzzaman. We live away from these spiritual people; our world is deprived of their colors. Islam is perceived by others by looking into our manners. As we depend on the Holy Qur'an for guidance, the Holy Qur'an depends upon sincerely devoted people to express its full potential. Even if the Qur'an is kept on high shelves in velvet covers but is not represented by people, then the Qur'an cannot speak for itself. Since its revelation, the Qur'an has been a guide for humanity in the

form of a materialized spirit. However, as you may see, sometimes its voice has been loud, while other times, it has been
silent, as if its mouth was zipped and it was locked in secret
chambers.[52]

In short, when representation was strong, communicating the
faith was also strong:

> Without conscious and strong-minded representatives, the
> Holy *Qur'an* experiences a pathetic situation. The perfect book
> can promulgate its message only through a perfect team of
> representatives. Unfortunately, because the world today lacks
> such representatives, many who study Islam are forced to view
> those who fail as representing the truth. A perfect team of rep-
> resentatives, a team that devotes itself completely to communi-
> cating God's name and to becoming a part of the religion, will
> be able to illustrate properly the ways in which the Qur'an
> might find expression. The main principle is not to intermedi-
> ate, or to get in the way of another person finding God on his
> or her own; rather, our goal is to merely provide an uncom-
> promising example of true faith. Each of us should strive to
> make people say, "There is no sign of lying on his face." We
> must show people the reality and make people think, "If their
> religion instills such depth of truth and morality, then their
> religion must not be false."[53]
>
> People who consider "communicating the faith" as their
> business can learn many lessons from the life of the Prophet.
> The only way to affect other people is to practice the message
> first. If you want to explain to someone about what it feels like
> to burst into tears for God, then you have to wake up at night
> and you have to weep until you wet your prayer mat. Only
> then will you see how your words the next day will make a
> tremendous impression. Otherwise, you may be slapped on
> your face, as in the verse, "Why do you say what you do not
> do?" (Saff 61:2).[54]
>
> [Believers who communicate the message] must pursue the
> same behavior they adopted while amongst people also when
> they are by themselves, and they must be sincere in all their
> behaviors. They must not contradict themselves in their per-
> sonal or social behaviors. Their nights must be as bright as
> their days, and their days must be so lucid as to illuminate the

sun. Any mistake they make out of carelessness must make them groan. They must feel ashamed to mention prayer in the morning if they have not performed the *tahajjud*[55] prayer at night. They must weep until they purify the sin they committed with their eyes. Any unlawful or doubtful food they ate must make their stomach ache for days and days, and they must feel any diversion as flames from the Hellfire.

Reflections and thoughts that are not practiced by individuals are not welcomed, regardless of how attractive and necessary they are. The words must be welcomed first in the hearts of the person uttering them. If the thought is not settled in one's heart, then it is impossible to expect it to be accepted by others.[56]

Exposing the internal dynamics of the Gülen movement and interpreting these in a systematic way, is not limited to this analysis. When we look at Gülen's discourse more closely, we observe other concepts such as humility (*tevazu*) and modesty (*mahviyet*); brotherhood (*kardeşlik*) and annihilation in friendship (*tefani*); material-spiritual benevolence (*himmet*) and advising each other what is good (*hayırhahlık*); connection with God (*Allah'la irtibat*) and becoming one with one's remembrances and prayers (*evrad ve ezkar ile bütünleşme*); being a person of heart (*gönül insanı olma*); abandoning one's spiritual prosperity (*füyuzat hislerinden feragat*); positive action (*müspet hareket*); etc.[57] We elaborated on only some of the features in order to give examples. This elaboration is no way a deep analysis. But I think that even this may give us some hints about the Gülen movement and its basic discourse. Before one can comment on the movement's action in society, these basic dynamics should be understood and taken into account. Such is the same for studying other Islamic movements, be they analyzed from a Muslim perspective or through social methods. The internal and spiritual dynamics of a movement gives life to its social existence at every movement; it spreads to the capillaries of individuals and to the social existence and identity of the movement as a whole. Ideals and social realities may contradict each other, but this generally stems from imbalances between thoughts and action. Sometimes, actions are at the front of thoughts and ideals, while sometimes, thoughts and ideals lead to actions. Observation of such imbalances may lead some to unjust critiques about the movement, or to some false descriptions or accusations.

This often happens when one Islamic movement critiques and evaluates another. Temporal developments may shape the discourse of a movement in its outward form on the basis of floating values. This may lead some people to speculate that a movement has strayed from internal/ideal principles. What is evident, however, is that variable values are necessary for flexibility and for occasional expansion. Variable values cannot determine ideal principles, but they may affect the movement when a new expansion is necessary. Obviously, change is not always something that every movement may desire all the time, and movements may not always need to renew or expand from their local milieu. This often leads to steadiness for some movements, and this steadiness must also be questioned. I argue, however, that variable values also display a capacity to adapt to a changing society and a capacity to produce new relations and values. A movement that does not possess this capacity will surely disappear. I hope my observation around "constants and variables" is not misinterpreted. The reason I utter this worry is because this issue designates a highly slippery ground. Further, it associates with loose and incurious observations and interpretations that we observe in modern political environments. Liberal readings often suggest that every change and development is inevitable. Our intent here is simply to disagree with an approach that suggests a sociological possibility for transformations without a base or parameters, one which idolizes all carnal egotistic pleasures and passion. Every interpretation and analysis must look at constant and dynamic values more closely. This is too often overlooked in the analysis of movements. Emotional and ideological readings trivialize everything and bear neither human nor moral concerns.

CONCLUDING REMARKS

One of the main difficulties in developing an analysis that traces a movement within its socio-cultural context is to determine the constants and variables of the movement. Once we view certain constants in the development of a movement, we then can begin our undertaking to analyze that movement.

The discourse of a movement generally forms from two elements: *constant* and *variable*. Constants represent the principal dynamics of a movement, while variables imply transitory interpretations and expansions. There is much to say about the Gülen movement. Our attempt has been only to elaborate its main parameters, and its religious dimension. This was a deliberate move. Our intent was to bring the cultural and social identity of the movement to the fore. Certainly Gülen's Islamic identity is a major aspect of his personality. There is no doubt that this identity surrounds his words and acts. A study which would trace religious traditions would give an opportunity to further understand the different religious sensitivities of the Gülen movement. In my analysis of the Gülen movement, I would say that I have tried to interpret every subject, filled with consciousness of my responsibility in the light of history. I hope the reader tolerates any deficiencies that originated from a shortage of knowledge and experience, as well as from my own opinions and interpretations. Effort is from us whereas success is possible only if God Almighty wills it so.

In conclusion, I would like to summarize my analysis about Fethullah Gülen and the Gülen movement in the following points:

1. The Gülen movement is not a political or ideological movement.

2. The Gülen movement is entirely a civil initiative.

3. The Gülen movement is an important experience that manifests the capacity and dynamism of Islam by creating rich social and cultural relations.

4. The Gülen movement has developed a new system for the delivery of humanitarian and social services.

5. The Gülen movement has a sharing structure that encompasses all segments of society.

6. The Gülen movement reconciles and combines people as it unites religious values and social ideals.

7. The Gülen movement does not emphasize individual capabilities, but rather makes its participants acquire a wide social identity and personality.

8. The Gülen movement is not a traditional *tariqa* organization, nor is it a secular movement in the modern sense.

9. The Gülen movement is a positive movement that values tolerance and affection; reconciliation and dialogue; and positive conduct in behavior and action.

10. The Gülen movement has neither material nor worldly expectations, nor does it have a hidden agenda to assume political power.

11. The Gülen movement is an altruistic and sacrificing movement; it strives to give to, not to take from, society.

NOTES

CHAPTER 1: M. FETHULLAH GÜLEN AND HIS MISSION

1   The first Abant Meeting took place on March 23, 1998, and the main theme was "Islam and Secularism." The themes of the subsequent meetings were "Religion, State, and Society (1999)," "Democratic Law State (2000)," "Pluralism and Societal Reconciliation (2001)," "Globalization (2002)," "War and Democracy (2003)," "Islam, Secularism, and Democracy: Turkish Experience (2004)," "Culture, Identity, and Religion during the Process of Turkish Membership to the EU (2004)," "New Quests in Education (2005)," "The Republic, Cultural Pluralism, and Europe (2006)," "Global Politics and the Future of the Middle East (2006)," "Turkish–Egyptian Talks: Islam, the West, and Modernization (2007)," and "Alevism in Historical, Cultural, Folkloric, and Current Dimensions (2007)."

2   See M. Fethullah Gülen, *The Statue of Our Souls*, NJ: The Light, Inc., 2005, p. 122, 145, 159; Gündem, Mehmet, "Interview with Fethullah Gülen," *Milliyet*, 21.01.2005 (http://en.fgulen.com/content/view/1924/14/).

3   These Sufi figures of Turkish history are considered to represent the most welcoming interpretation of Islam. Their poetry and exemplary life stories have been narrated generation after generation.

4   See Gülen, *Ölçü veya Yoldaki Işıklar*, Istanbul: Nil Yayınları, 2004 p. 107–108, 192; *Yeşeren Düşünceler*, Istanbul: Nil Yayınları, 2005, p. 110, 142; *Işığın Göründüğü Ufuk*, Istanbul: Nil Yayınları, 2002, p. 35; *Örnekleri Kendinden Bir Hareket*, Istanbul: Nil Yayınları, 2004, p. 117; *Fasıldan Fasıla* Vol. 2, Izmir: Nil Yayınları, 1998, p. 127; *Sohbet-i Canan*, Istanbul: Gazeteciler ve Yazarlar Vakfı, 2004, p. 125.

5   Throughout this book, *tolerance* is translated for the lack of better word as the equivalent of the Turkish word, *hoşgörü*, which has a broader connotation in Turkish than tolerance in English. While tolerance implies a degree of forbearance, here it should be understood as accepting people as they are.

6   See Yusuf Qaradawi, *Ghayru'l Muslimin fi'l Mujtamai'l Islami*, p. 10.

CHAPTER 2: SOCIOLOGICAL PERSPECTIVE

1   See Ali Köse, edited by, *Sekülerizm Sorgulanıyor*, Istanbul: Ufuk Yayınları, 2002, pp. 41–42.

2   See ibid, p. 77; P. L. Berger and T. Luckmann, *The Social Construction of Reality: A Treatise in the Sociology of Knowledge*, Garden City, NY: Anchor Books, 1966.

3   These authors still comprise the foundational body of work as "literary masters" required for students in the West who major in English, the classics, history, and political science.

4   See Jocelyne Cesari and John Esposito, *İslam'dan Korkmalı mı*, Istanbul: Birey Yayıncılık, 1999, p. 9.

5   *Asr-ı Saadet* refers to the time of the Prophet Muhammad, peace be upon him.

6   See Gülen, *Kendi Dünyamıza Doğru*, Istanbul: Nil Yayınları, 2005, p. 185; *Asrın Getirdiği Tereddütler*, Nil Yayınları, Izmir: 1998, Vol. 4, pp. 164–7; "Dar Bir Çerçeveden Din ve Vicdan Hürriyeti," *Yeni Ümit*, No. 64, April 2004; *Fasıldan Fasıla*, Vol. 2, p. 50; *İnancın Gölgesinde*, Istanbul: Nil Yayınları, 2002, Vol. 2, p. 27.

CHAPTER 3: CULTURAL PERSPECTIVE

1   After the establishment of the Republic, the Turkish language has undergone an enormous transformation in which many words of Arabic and Persian origins have been removed (or attempted to have been removed) from the lexicon with new words being coined to fill the void. Nevertheless, a great deal of the older vocabulary is still in use. As a consequence, there are now two words—old and new—referring to the same concept, with a slight difference in nuance; the older word is used in a more religious context, whereas the new vocabulary is preferred for secular references. The author is referring to this when he uses the combination of *ilim–bilim* for "science," *münevver–aydın* for "learned," and *mütefekkir–entelektüel* for "intellectual."

2   For a similar tension in the Arab modernization, see Ibrahim Abu-Rabi, *Intellectual Origins of Islamic Resurgence in the Modern Arab World*, Albany: State University of New York Press, 1996.

3   See Thomas S. Kuhn, *Bilimsel Devrimlerin Yapısı*, Istanbul: Kırmızı Yayıncılık, 2006. Originally published as *The Structure of Scientific Revolutions*, Chicago: University of Chicago Press, 1996; Immanuel Wallerstein, *Bildiğimiz*

Dünyanın Sonu, Istanbul: Metis Yayınları, 2000. Originally published as *The End of the World As We Know It*, University of Minnesota Press, Minneapolis: 2001; Paul Feyerabend, *Özgür Bir Toplumda Bilim*; *Yönteme Karşı*, Istanbul: Ayrıntı Yayınları, 1999. Originally published as *Against Method*, London: Verso, 1993.

4   See Wallerstein, p. 10.

5   For more information see Steven Shapin, *Bilimsel Devrim*, Istanbul: İzdüşüm Yayınları, 2000, p. 154. Originally published as *The Scientific Revolution*, Chicago: University of Chicago Press, 1998.

6   Ibid.

7   Ibid.

8   Feyerabend, p. 100.

9   Ibid., p. 103.

10   Shapin, 2000.

11   Ibid.

12   Ibid.

13   İrfan Yılmaz et al., *Yeni Bir Bakış Açısıyla İlim ve Din*, Izmir: Nil Yayınları, 1998, p. 10.

14   Ibid., p. 11.

15   Ibid., p. 16.

16   Ibid., p. 17.

17   Ibid., p. 17.

18   Ibid., p. 22.

19   Ibid., pp. 27–30.

20   Shapin, 2000, p. 82.

21   Gülen, *Günler Baharı Soluklarken*, Istanbul: Nil Yayınları, 2002, p. 17.

22   Ibid., p. 17.

23   Ibid., pp. 18–19.

24   Ibid., pp. 98–99.

25   Ibid., pp. 71–72.

26   Gülen, *Kendi Dünyamıza Doğru*, p. 67; *Günler Baharı Soluklarken*, pp. 70, 83.

27   Gülen, *Kendi Dünyamıza Doğru*, pp. 93, 130, 194; *Ruhumuzun Heykelini Dikerken*, Istanbul: Nil Yayınları, 2002, p. 32; *Gurbet Ufukları*, Istanbul: Gazeteciler ve Yazarlar Vakfı, 2004, p. 157; *Örnekleri Kendinden Bir Hareket*, p. 50; "Kur'an-ı Kerim ve İlmi Hakikatler," *Yeni Ümit*, No. 16, April 1992.

28   Gülen, *Yeşeren Düşünceler*, pp. 105, 179–181. See also, Gülen, *Ruhumuzun Heykelini Dikerken*, p. 114; *Beyan*, Istanbul: Nil Yayınları, 2008, pp. 88,

105; *Zamanın Altın Dilimi*, Istanbul: Nil Yayınları, 2002, p. 19; "Işık–Karanlık Devr-i Daimi," *Sızıntı*, No. 298, November 2003.

29 Gülen, *Işığın Göründüğü Ufuk*, p. 10.

30 Ibid.

31 Ibid.

32 Ibid.

33 Ibid, p. 12.

34 See Gülen, *Çağ ve Nesil*, Nil Yayınları, Izmir: 2002, pp. 115–8; *Günler Baharı Soluklarken*, pp. 70, 84, 90; *Işığın Göründüğü Ufuk*, pp. 102–7.

35 See Gülen, *Yeşeren Düşünceler*, pp. 172–188; *Işığın Göründüğü Ufuk*, pp. 16–20, 57, 65–70; *Ruhumuzun Heykelini Dikerken*, pp. 36, 97; *Kendi Dünyamıza Doğru*, pp. 19–25, 66; *Beyan*, 127; *Sohbet-i Canan*, p. 66; "Hakikat Aşkı," *Sızıntı*, No. 304, May 2004; "İlim ve Araştırma Aşkı," *Sızıntı*, No. 305, June 2004.

36 Gülen, *Kendi Dünyamıza Doğru*, pp. 73–85. "The Qur'an teaches us this way and it defines 'to be reasonable' as to relate the thought to the infinity."

37 Ibid.

38 For a detailed account on Nursi's exegesis, see Ibrahim Abu-Rabi, *Islam at the Crossroads: On the Life and Thought of Bediuzzaman Said Nursi*, Albany: State University of New York Press, 2003.

39 Gülen, *Kendi Dünyamıza Doğru*, pp. 73–85.

40 See also, ibid., pp. 130, 142; *Sohbet-i Canan*, p. 192.

41 Gülen, *Kalbin Zümrüt Tepeleri*, Vol. 2, Istanbul: Nil Yayınları, 2001, p. 19; *Prizma*, Vol. 2, Istanbul: Nil Yayınları, 2002, p. 66.

42 Gülen, *Fasıldan Fasıla*, Vol. 3, Izmir: Nil Yayınları, 1998, p. 194.

43 Gülen, *Kendi Dünyamıza Doğru*, p. 142.

44 Ibid.

45 Cemal Uşak, *Küresel Barışa Doğru: Kozadan Kelebeğe*, Vol. 3, Istanbul: Gazeteciler ve Yazarlar Vakfı Yayınları, 2003, p. 55.

46 Definitions like Turkish Islam—even though it is usually used in figurative sense—are not true, for Islam is universal, and no one type as practiced by any nation is superior to others.

47 Armağan and Ünal, p. 87.

48 For the intellectual roots of Turkish Muslimness, see Etga Ugur, "Intellectual Roots of 'Turkish Islam' and Approaches to the Turkish Model," *Journal of Muslim Minority Affairs*, 24 (2): 327–45, 2004.

49 Pietism is the discourse that places individual morality as the essential element of religiosity. Weber's *The Protestant Ethic and the Spirit of Capitalism* discusses pietism extensively.

50 See Eyüp Can, *Fethullah Gülen ile Ufuk Turu*, Istanbul: A.D., 1996, p. 35; Hulusi Turgut, "Nur Hareketi," *Sabah*, January 15, 1997; Gülen, *Fasıldan Fasıla*, Vol. 2, p. 53; *Ruhumuzun Heykelini Dikerken*, 115; *Prizma*, Vol. 3, pp. 72–3; www.herkul.org/Kırık Testi "Meçhul Kahramanlar," April 18, 2005.

51 See the Qur'an, Anbiya 21:105.

52 Gülen, *The Statue of Our Souls*, pp. 59–62.

53 See Gülen, *Işığın Göründüğü Ufuk*, pp. 75, 213; *Örnekleri Kendinden Bir Hareket*, pp. 114, 119.

54 See Bekim Agai, "The Gülen Movement's Islamic Ethic of Education." *Critique: Critical Middle Eastern Studies* 2002: 11 (1), pp. 27–47.

55 Gülen, *Örnekleri Kendinden Bir Hareket*, p. 117; *Ruhumuzun Heykelini Dikerken*, p. 122; *Yeşeren Düşünceler*, p. 156; *Kendi Dünyamıza Doğru*, p. 50; "İslam Dünyası," *Sızıntı*, No. 302, March 2004.

56 For a detailed analysis on the Abant meetings, see Etga Ugur, "Religion as a Source of Social Capital? The Gülen Movement in the Public Sphere," in *Muslim World in Transition: Contributions of the Gülen Movement: International Conference Proceedings*, ed. Ihsan Yilmaz, London: Leeds Metropolitan University Press, 2007.

57 The writings of Thomas Michel, who is the Secretary of Vatican Secreteriat for Inter-Religious Dialogue, are very good examples to prove this fact. See, for instance, Thomas Michel, "Sufism and Modernity in the Thought of Fethullah Gülen," *The Muslim World* 2005, 95 (3): 341–58.

58 Gülen, *The Statue of Our Souls*, p. 60.

59 Ibid., p. 59.

62 Ibid., pp. 59–60.

61 See Elisabeth Özdalga, "Worldly Asceticism in Islamic Casting: Fethullah Gülen's Inspired Piety and Activism." *Critique: Critical Middle Eastern Studies* 2000: 17, 84–104.

62 Gülen, *The Statue of Our Souls*, pp. 19–24.

63 See Gülen, *Buhranlar Anaforunda İnsan*, Istanbul: Nil Yayınları, 2002, p. 53; *Yeşeren Düşünceler*, pp. 43–44; *Kendi Dünyamıza Doğru*, pp. 26–35; *Zamanın Altın Dilimi*, pp. 157–160; *Ruhumuzun Heykelini Dikerken*, pp. 31, 91; *Işığın Göründüğü Ufuk*, p. 106.

64 See Keith Jenkins, *Tarihi Yeniden Düşünmek*, Istanbul: Dost Yayınları, 1997, pp. 29–31. Originally published as *Re-Thinking History*, London: Routledge, 2003.

65 Gülen, *The Statue of Our Souls*, p. 19.

66 Ibid.

67 Ibid., p. 21.

68 Ibid., p. 21.

69 Ibid.

70 Ibid.

71 Ibid.

72 Reform is a word that must be used with caution. Throughout the text, we use this word to correspond *islah*. It is by no means intended with this usage to refer to the Reformation experience of Christianity, which targeted the essential elements of the Church. "Reform" for *islah* is written as it is. When we refer to attempts directed toward the essentials of Islam, which is unacceptable in the case of Islamic experience, we spell "re-form" with a dash or Reformation with a capitalized initial.

73 Please note that in this context "re-form" is loaded with a different meaning than "reform" which we use for *islah*. The former connotes to a colossal change by reconstructing the essentials of Islam, however, *islah* implies any social activity that is geared toward the proliferation of the society while preserving the essentials as the main source of reference.

74 See Gülen, *Buhranlar Anaforunda İnsan*, pp. 54, 63; *Yitirilmiş Cennete Doğru*, pp. 28, 130; *Yeşeren Düşünceler*, pp. 130–1, 157; *Işığın Göründüğü Ufuk*, pp. 20, 58, 74, 80, 107, 131, 142; *Ruhumuzun Heykelini Dikerken*, pp. 87, 107, 112, 115, 132; *Örnekleri Kendinden Bir Hareket*, pp. 89, 120.

75 Can, p. 65. See also Gülen, *Fasıldan Fasıla*, Vol. 3, p. 190.

76 Ibid, p. 66.

77 Ibid. See also Gülen, *Çağ ve Nesil*, p. 122; *Zamanın Altın Dilimi*, pp. 29, 48, 53, 54, 68, 69; *Yitirilmiş Cennete Doğru*, p. 43; *Yeşeren Düşünceler*, pp. 88–92, 57, 103; *Işığın Göründüğü Ufuk*, pp. 90–95, 120, 98; *Beyan*, p. 23; *Örnekleri Kendinden Bir Hareket*, pp. 67, 104; "Faniliklerle Kuşatılan Ruhlar," *Sızıntı*, No. 311, December 2004.

78 For more information see Bayram Kodaman, *Abdülhamit Devri Eğitim Sistemi*, Istanbul: Ötüken Yayınları, 1999, p. 11.

79 In Turkish, "college" (*kolej*) does not refer to an institution of higher learning, but to private mostly secondary schools. This usage is also valid in some case in Britain and Canada. We kept this term to distinguish the schools inspired by Gülen from *madrasa*, *maktab*, or a state school, all of which fall into the category of school in one way.

80 Can, pp. 71–89. See also Gülen, *The Statue of Our Souls*, p. 41; *Işığın Göründüğü Ufuk*, p. 71; *Fasıldan Fasıla*, Vol. 3, pp. 198–199, 122; www. herkul.org/Kırık Testi/ "Devlet Kutsanmamalı ama..." September 5, 2004.

81 Ibid.

82 Ibid.

83 Ibid.

84 Ibid., pp. 84–85. See also Gülen, *Key Concepts in the Practice of Sufism*, Vol. 2, NJ: The Light, Inc., 2004, p. 135; *Fasıldan Fasıla*, Vol. 2, p. 75; *Prizma*, Vol. 3, p. 150, 167.

85 Ibid., p. 83. See also Gülen, *Prizma*, Vol. 1, p. 74; *Buhranlar Anaforunda İnsan*, pp. 43, 100; *Günler Baharı Soluklarken*, p. 153–161; *Işığın Göründüğü Ufuk*, p. 30; *Fasıldan Fasıla*, Vol. 1, Izmir: Nil Yayınları, 1997, p. 65, Vol. 4, p. 29; *Ölçü veya Yoldaki Işıklar*, p. 100; "Hak Karşısındaki Konumu ve Duruşuyla İnsan," *Sızıntı*, No. 301, February 2004.

86 See Mehmet Gündem, *Fethullah Gülen ile 11 Gün*, Istanbul: Alfa, 2005, p. 94; Gülen, *Sohbet-i Canan*, pp. 105–107.

87 See Gülen, *Buhranlar Anaforunda İnsan*, p. 110; *Zamanın Altın Dilimi*, p. 157; *Sonsuz Nur*, Vol. 1, Istanbul: Nil Yayınları, 2002, pp. 202–204; *Fasıldan Fasıla*, Vol. 4, Istanbul: 2002, p. 29; *Prizma*, Vol. 4, p. 96; *Ruhumuzun Heykelini Dikerken*, pp. 8, 36; *Örnekleri Kendinden Bir Hareket*, pp. 95, 115; *Beyan*, p. 110; *Kendi Dünyamıza Doğru*, p. 43, 68, 77, 114; *Kırık Testi*, Vol. 1, Istanbul: Gazeteciler ve Yazarlar Vakfı, 2004, p. 175; "Şafaklar Üst Üsteydi", *Sızıntı*, No. 307, August 2004; www. herkul.org, Kırık Testi "Kültür Müslümanlığı ve Tahkiki İman" December 12, 2004.

88 Traditionally, teachers have always been highly respected in the Turkish culture. However, teaching did not use to be a popular occupation until recently due to low salaries and very few benefits. Regulations are changing rapidly to improve their conditions.

89 For a useful analysis, see Zeki Saritoprak, "Fethullah Gülen: A Sufi in His own Way." In *Turkish Islam and the Secular State: The Gülen Movement*, edited by Hakan Yavuz and John Esposito, NY: Syracuse University Press, 2003.

90 Nomadic community refers to the Companions of the Prophet Muhammad, peace be upon him.

91 Gülen, *Çağ ve Nesil*, pp. 110–114.

92 Ibid., pp. 101–104.

93 Gülen, *Yitirilmiş Cennete Doğru*, p. 125.

94 Gülen, *Buhranlar Anaforunda İnsan*, p. 101.

95 Gülen, *Çağ ve Nesil*, p. 107.

96 Gülen, *Buhranlar Anaforunda İnsan*, p. 88.

97 Gülen, *The Statue of Our Souls*, pp. 101–2.

98 Gülen, *Kendi Dünyamıza Doğru*, p. 58.

CHAPTER 4: RELIGIOUS PERSPECTIVE

1   Ajluni, *Kashf al-Khafa*, 1/127, Tabari, *History*, 2/146.

2   "Or is it the law of the (pagan) Ignorance that they seek (to be judged and ruled by)? Who is better than God as law-giver and judge for a people seeking certainty (and authoritative knowledge)?" (Maidah 5:50).

3   "Help one another in goodness and piety, and do not help one another in sinful, iniquitous acts and hostility" (Maidah 5:2). See also Baqara 2:148.

4   ". . . Who impedes the doing of good (preventing himself and others), and who exceeds all bounds (of right and decency), and who is lost in doubts and implants doubts (in others) . . ." (Qaf 50:25). See also Qalam 68:12, Maun 107:7.

5   Gülen, *Yeşeren Düşünceler*, p. 186.

6   Ibid.

7   Ibid.

8   Tirmidhi, *Sifat al Qiyama*, 55; Ibn Maja, *Fitan*, 23.

9   Gülen, *Yeşeren Düşünceler*, pp. 186–187.

10   Gülen, *Yeşeren Düşünceler*, pp. 187–188.

11   See Ebu'l Ala Afifi, *Tasavvuf*, Istanbul: İz Yayıncılık, 1999, p. 20–21.

12   See, ibid., p. 92.

13   Ibid., p. 92.

14   Ibid., pp. 81–115.

15   Seyyed Hossein Nasr, *The Heart of Islam: Enduring Values for Humanity*, NY: HarperSanFrancisco, 2004, pp. 64–65.

16   See, Gülen, *Sonsuz Nur*, Vol. 2, pp. 472–484; *Örnekleri Kendinden Bir Hareket*, p. 40; *Işığın Göründüğü Ufuk*, p. 193; *Kur'an'dan İdrake Yansıyanlar*, Vol. 2, Istanbul: Zaman Yayınları, 2000, pp. 307–313; *Kalbin Zümrüt Tepeleri*, Vol. 1, p. 72; *Kendi Dünyamıza Doğru*, p. 157; *Fasıldan Fasıla*, Vol. 4, p. 109.

17   See Bediüzzaman Said Nursi, *The Words*, Thirty-second Word, Fifth Indication, NJ: The Light, Inc., 2005, p. 632.

18   See An'am 6:32; Ankabut 29:64; Muhammad 47:36; Hadid 11:20.

19   See Gülen, *Kur'an'dan İdrake Yansıyanlar*, Vol. 2, pp. 307–313; *Kırık Testi*, p. 203.

20   See Gülen, *Key Concepts in the Practice of Sufism*, Vol. 1, p. 19; *Buhranlar Anaforunda İnsan*, p. 129. See also, "Sefer," *Sızıntı*, No. 250, November 1999; "Halvet–Celvet," *Sızıntı*, No. 253, February 2000.

21   See, Afifi, p. 116.

22   Tirmidhi, *Fitan*, 7.

23 Gülen, *Fasıldan Fasıla*, Vol. 1, p. 171–2.

24 Ibid., p. 172.

25 Ibid., p. 173.

26 Ibid., p. 174.

27 See the Qur'an, Isra 17:44; Juma 62:1; Taghabun 64:1; Hadid 57:1; Hashr 59:1, 24; Saf 61:1. ". . . since the globe utters Divine glorifications to the number of its realms of beings, with tongues to the number of the members of those species, and the parts, leaves, and fruits of those members, surely there will be an appointed angel with forty thousand heads and forty thousand tongues in each head, each of which will utter forty thousand Divine glorifications, which will know that splendid, unconscious, innate worship, represent it consciously, and offer it to the Divine Court, as the Bringer of Sure News informed us absolutely correctly" (Nursi, *Rays*, Eleventh Topic, Istanbul: Sözler Publications, 2002, p. 283).

28 See Gülen, *Prizma*, Vol. 4, p. 76; *İnancın Gölgesinde*, Vol. 2, p. 174; *Ruhumuzun Heykelini Dikerken*, p. 35; *Prizma*, Vol. 1, p. 128, Vol. 3, pp. 12–13; *Kırık Testi*, p. 121–126; *Gurbet Ufukları*, pp. 18, 89.

29 See Gülen, *Örnekleri Kendinden Bir Hareket*, pp. 112, 120; *Günler Baharı Soluklarken*, p. 86; *Işığın Göründüğü Ufuk*, pp. 138, 261; *İrşad Ekseni*, Istanbul: Nil Yayınları, 2001, p. 215; *Çağ ve Nesil*, p. 22.

30 See, http://tr.fgulen.com/content/view/13315/3/

31 See Gülen, *Fatiha Üzerine Mülahazalar*, Istanbul: Nil Yayınları, 2002, p. 189–190; *Ölçü veya Yoldaki Işıklar*, p. 101; *Kalbin Zümrüt Tepeleri*, Vol. 1, p. 113; *Kırık Testi*, pp. 212, 215; *Sohbet-i Canan*, p. 166; "Hak Karşısında Konumu ve Duruşuyla İnsan," *Sızıntı*, No. 301, February 2004; "İnsanın Konumu," *Sızıntı*, No. 302, March 2004; www.herkul. org, *Kırık Testi*, "Ayaklarımızı Kaydırma Allah'ım," March 7, 2005; www.herkul.org, *Kırık Testi*, "Meçhul Kahramanlar," April 18, 2005; www.herkul.org, *Kırık Testi*, "En Önemli Vazife," September 2004.

32 Gülen, *İ'lay-i Kelimetullah veya Cihad*, Istanbul: Nil Yayınları, 2001.

33 Gülen, *Yitirilmiş Cennete Doğru*, p. 128.

34 Gülen, *Işığın Göründüğü Ufuk*, p. 138.

35 Ibid., p. 142.

36 Gülen, *Örnekleri Kendinden Bir Hareket*, p. 218–219.

37 Gülen, *Ölçü veya Yoldaki Işıklar*, p. 108.

38 Ibid., p. 121.

39 Gülen, *The Statue of Our Souls*, p. 95.

40 Gülen, *Toward a Global Civilization of Love and Tolerance*, NJ: The Light, Inc., 2006, pp. 21, 23.

41   Gülen, *Çağ ve Nesil*, p. 143

42   Gülen, *Işığın Göründüğü Ufuk*, p. 261.

43   Gülen, *The Statue of Our Souls*, p. 97.

44   See Gülen, *Örnekleri Kendinden Bir Hareket*, pp. 185, 187, 189; *Beyan*, pp. 48, 55, 113, 142.

45   Gülen, *Toward a Global Civilization of Love and Tolerance*, pp. 100–103.

46   Gülen, *İrşad Ekseni*, pp. 188–189.

47   Gülen, *Buhranlar Anaforunda İnsan*, pp. 38–39. See also, *Işığın Göründüğü Ufuk*, p. 100; *Ölçü veya Yoldaki Işıklar*, pp. 147, 199–204; *Fasıldan Fasıla*, Vol. 1, p. 180, Vol. 3, p. 130; *Çağ ve Nesil*, p. 10; *Beyan*, pp. 60, 143; "Işık–Karanlık Devr-i Daimi," *Sızıntı*, No. 298, November 2003.

48   Gülen, *Pearls of Wisdom*, NJ: The Light, Inc., 2006, p. 105.

49   Gülen, *Işığın Göründüğü Ufuk*, p. 4.

50   Gülen, *Sohbet-i Canan*, p. 96.

51   Ibid., 98–99.

52   Ibid., pp. 99–100.

53   Ibid., pp. 103–4.

54   Gülen, *Sonsuz Nur*, Vol. 1, p. 244.

55   A voluntary prayer observed late at night.

56   Gülen, *İrşad Ekseni*, pp. 134–136.

57   Gülen, *Prizma*, Vol. 1, pp. 12–15; Vol. 3, pp. 50–52, 143–146; *Çağ ve Nesil*, pp. 21, 57–60; *Yeşeren Düşünceler*, pp. 19–22; *Işığın Göründüğü Ufuk*, p. 194; *Ruhumuzun Heykelini Dikerken*, p. 86; *Kalbin Zümrüt Tepeleri*, Vol. 1, pp. 146, 219; Vol. 2, p. 97; *Kırık Testi*, p. 137.

BIBLIOGRAPHY

Abu-Rabi, Ibrahim. *Intellectual Origins of Islamic Resurgence in the Modern Arab World*, Albany: State University of New York Press, 1996.

———— *Islam at the Crossroads: On the Life and Thought of Bediuzzaman Said Nursi*, Albany: State University of New York Press, 2003.

Afifi, Ebu'l Ala, *Tasavvuf*, Istanbul: İz Yayıncılık, 1999.

Agai, Bekim. "The Gülen Movement's Islamic Ethic of Education." *Critique: Critical Middle Eastern Studies*, 2002.

Ajluni, Ismail ibn Muhammad al-Jarrahi. *Kashf al-Khafa wa mudhil al-ilbas*, Vol. 1, 2, Beirut: Muassasa al-Risala, 1405 AH.

Berger, P. L. and T. Luckmann, *The Social Construction of Reality: A Treatise in the Sociology of Knowledge*, Garden City, NY: Anchor Books, 1966.

Can, Eyüp. *Fethullah Gülen ile Ufuk Turu*, Istanbul: A.D., 1996.

Cesari, Jocelyne and John Esposito. *İslam'dan Korkmalı mı*, Istanbul: Birey Yayıncılık, 1999.

Feyerabend, Paul. *Özgür Bir Toplumda Bilim; Yönteme Karşı*, Istanbul: Ayrıntı Yayınları, 1999. Originally published as *Against Method*, London: Verso, 1993.

Gülen, M. Fethullah. *Asrın Getirdiği Tereddütler*, Izmir: Nil Yayınları, 1998, Vol. 4.

———— *Beyan*, Istanbul: Nil Yayınları, 2008.

———— *Buhranlar Anaforunda İnsan*, Istanbul: Nil Yayınları, 2002.

———— *Çağ ve Nesil*, Izmir: Nil Yayınları, 2002.

———— "Dar Bir Çerçeveden Din ve Vicdan Hürriyeti," *Yeni Ümit*, No. 64, April 2004.

———— "Faniliklerle Kuşatılan Ruhlar," *Sızıntı*, No. 311, December 2004.

———— *Fasıldan Fasıla* Vol. 1, Izmir: Nil Yayınları, 1997.

———— *Fasıldan Fasıla* Vol. 2, Izmir: Nil Yayınları, 1998.

———— *Fasıldan Fasıla* Vol. 3, Izmir: Nil Yayınları, 1998.

———— *Fasıldan Fasıla* Vol. 4, Istanbul: Nil Yayınları, 2002.

———— *Fatiha Üzerine Mülahazalar*, Istanbul: Nil Yayınları, 2002.

———— *Gurbet Ufukları*, Istanbul: Gazeteciler ve Yazarlar Vakfı, 2004.

———— *Günler Baharı Soluklarken*, Istanbul: Nil Yayınları, 2002.

———— "Hak Karşısındaki Konumu ve Duruşuyla İnsan," *Sızıntı*, No. 301, February 2004.

———— "Hakikat Aşkı," *Sızıntı*, No. 304, May 2004.

———— "Halvet-Celvet," *Sızıntı*, No. 253, February 2000.

———— *Işığın Göründüğü Ufuk*, Istanbul: Nil Yayınları, 2002.

———— "Işık–Karanlık Devr-i Daimi," *Sızıntı*, No. 298, November 2003.

———— *İ'lay-i Kelimetullah veya Cihad*, Istanbul: Nil Yayınları, 2001.

———— "İlim ve Araştırma Aşkı," *Sızıntı*, No. 305, June 2004.

———— *İnancın Gölgesinde*, Istanbul: Nil Yayınları, 2002.

———— "İnsanın Konumu," *Sızıntı*, No. 302, March 2004.

———— *İrşad Ekseni*, Istanbul: Nil Yayınları, 2001.

———— "İslam Dünyası," *Sızıntı*, No. 302, March 2004.

———— *Kalbin Zümrüt Tepeleri*, Vol. 2, Istanbul: Nil Yayınları, 2001.

———— *Kendi Dünyamıza Doğru*, Istanbul: Nil Yayınları, 2005.

———— *Key Concepts in the Practice of Sufism*, Vol. 2, The Light, Inc., NJ: 2004.

———— *Kırık Testi*, Vol. 1, Istanbul: Gazeteciler ve Yazarlar Vakfı, 2004.

———— *Kur'an'dan İdrake Yansıyanlar*, Vol. 2, Istanbul: Zaman Yayınları, 2000.

———— "Kur'an-ı Kerim ve İlmi Hakikatler," *Yeni Ümit*, No. 16, April 1992.

———— *Ölçü veya Yoldaki Işıklar*, Istanbul: Nil Yayınları, 2004.

———— *Örnekleri Kendinden Bir Hareket*, Istanbul: Nil Yayınları, 2004.

———— *Pearls of Wisdom*, NJ: The Light, Inc., 2006.

———— *Prizma*, Vol. 2, Istanbul: Nil Yayınları, 2002.

———— *Ruhumuzun Heykelini Dikerken*, Istanbul: Nil Yayınları, 2002.

———— "Sefer," *Sızıntı*, No. 250, November 1999.

———— *Sohbet-i Canan*, Istanbul: Gazeteciler ve Yazarlar Vakfı, 2004.

———— "Şafaklar Üst Üsteydi", *Sızıntı*, No. 307, August 2004.

———— *The Statue of Our Souls*, NJ: The Light, Inc., 2005.

———— *Toward a Global Civilization of Love and Tolerance*, NJ: The Light, Inc., 2006.

———— *Yeşeren Düşünceler*, Istanbul: Nil Yayınları, 2005.

———— *Zamanın Altın Dilimi*, Istanbul: Nil Yayınları, 2002.

Gündem, Mehmet. *Fethullah Gülen ile 11 Gün*, Istanbul: Alfa, 2005.

Ibn Maja, Muhammad b. Yazid al-Kazwini, *Fitan, al-Sunan*, Vol. 1–2, Second edition, Istanbul: Çağrı Yayınları, 1992.

Jenkins, Keith. *Tarihi Yeniden Düşünmek*, Istanbul: Dost Yayınları, 1997, pp. 29-31. Originally published as *Re-Thinking History*, London: Routledge, 2003.

Kodaman, Bayram. *Abdülhamit Devri Eğitim Sistemi*, Ötüken Yayınları, Istanbul: 1999.

Köse, Ali (ed.), *Sekülerizm Sorgulanıyor*, Istanbul: Ufuk Yayınları, 2002.

Kuhn, Thomas S. *Bilimsel Devrimlerin Yapısı*, Istanbul: Kırmızı Yayıncılık, 2006. Originally published as *The Structure of Scientific Revolutions*, Chicago: University of Chicago Press, 1996.

Michel, Thomas. "Sufism and Modernity in the Thought of Fethullah Gülen." *The Muslim World* 2005, 95 (3): 341-58.

Nasr, Seyyed Hossein. *The Heart of Islam: Enduring Values for Humanity*, NY: HarperSanFrancisco, 2004.

Nursi, Bediüzzaman Said. *The Rays*, Eleventh Topic, Istanbul: Sözler Publications, 2002.

———— *The Words*, Thirty-second Word, Fifth Indication, NJ: The Light, Inc. 2005.

Özdalga, Elisabeth. "Worldly Asceticism in Islamic Casting: Fethullah Gülen's Inspired Piety and Activism." *Critique: Critical Middle Eastern Studies* 2000: 17, 84-104.

Qaradawi, Yusuf. *Ghayru'l Muslimin fi'l Mujtamai'l Islami*.

Saritoprak, Zeki. "Fethullah Gülen: A Sufi in His own Way." In *Turkish Islam and the Secular State: The Gülen Movement*, edited by Hakan Yavuz and John Esposito, NY: Syracuse University Press, 2003.

Shapin, Steven. *Bilimsel Devrim*, Istanbul: İzdüşüm Yayınları, 2000. Originally published as *The Scientific Revolution*, Chicago: University of Chicago Press, 1998.

Tabari, Muhammad b. Jarir b. Yazid b. Halid. *Tarih al-Tabari*, Vol. 1-4, Beirut: Dar al-Kutub al-Ilmiyya, 1407 AH.

Tirmidhi, Abu Isa Muhammad b. Isa b. Savra, *Sifat al Qiyama, al-Jami al-Sahih*, Vol. 1-5, Second Edition, Istanbul: Çağrı Yayınları, 1992.

Turgut, Hulusi. "Nur Hareketi," *Sabah*, January 15, 1997.

Ugur, Etga. "Intellectual Roots of 'Turkish Islam' and Approaches to the Turkish Model," *Journal of Muslim Minority Affairs*, 24 (2): 327-45, 2004.

———— "Religion as a Source of Social Capital? The Gülen Movement in the Public Sphere," in *Muslim World in Transition: Contributions of the*

Gülen Movement: International Conference Proceedings, ed. Ihsan Yilmaz, Leeds Metropolitan University Press, 2007.

Unal, Ali. *The Qur'an with Annotated Interpretation in Modern English*, NJ: The Light, Inc., 2006.

Uşak, Cemal, *Küresel Barışa Doğru: Kozadan Kelebeğe*, Vol. 3, Istanbul: Gazeteciler ve Yazarlar Vakfı Yayınları, 2003.

Wallerstein, Immanuel. *Bildiğimiz Dünyanın Sonu*, Istanbul, Metis Yayınları, 2000. Originally published as *The End of the World As We Know It*, University of Minnesota Press, Minnesota: 2001

Weber, Max, *The Protestant Ethic and the Spirit of Capitalism*. Translated by Talcott Parsons. New York: Dover Publications, 2003

Yılmaz, İrfan et al., *Yeni Bir Bakış Açısıyla İlim ve Din*, Nil Yayınları, Izmir, 1998.

INDEX